THE SPIRIT OF REVIVAL
A CONTRITE AND HUMBLE SPIRIT

FOR THE GLORY OF THE LORD
PASTOR SCOTT MARKLE

Shepherding the Flock Ministries
7971 Washington St. ❖ Melvin, MI 48454
(810) 378-5323
www.shepherdingtheflock.com

Copyright © 2014 by Pastor Scott Markle. All Scripture quotations are from the King James Version.

The Spirit of Revival:
A Contrite and Humble Spirit
(Second Edition)
by Pastor Scott Markle

Printed in the United States of America

ISBN 978-0692328934

All rights reserved solely by the author. The author guarantees all contents are original and do not infringe upon the legal rights of any other person or work. No part of this book may be reproduced, stored in a retrieval system, or transmitted in any form or by any means – electronic, mechanical, photocopy, recording, or otherwise – without written permission of the publisher, except for brief quotations in printed reviews.

Shepherding the Flock Ministries
7971 Washington St.
Melvin, MI 48454
(810) 378-5323
www.shepherdingtheflock.com

DEDICATION

First and foremost,
To the indwelling Holy Spirit of God,
Who convicts me of my sinfulness
That I might humbly repent thereof,
And who convicts me of my weakness
That I might humbly depend upon Christ,
All that I might be changed from glory to glory
Into the image of my Lord and Savior Jesus Christ.

Furthermore,
To my fellow believers in Christ,
Oh how I pray that we might come to the place
Of a truly broken and contrite heart,
That our Lord might revive us again spiritually,
That we might know the joy and peace
Of His blessed fellowship!
Then let us not return unto the folly of our sin.

TABLE OF CONTENTS

Preface: Revival NOW!..ix

Isaiah 57:15-21

Chapter 1: Thus Saith the High and Lofty One 17

Chapter 2: With Him of a Contrite and Humble Spirit 25

Chapter 3: To Revive the Spirit of the Humble 33

Chapter 4: To Revive the Heart of the Contrite 41

Chapter 5: No Peace, Saith My God, to the Wicked 49

James 4:1-10

Chapter 6: Draw Nigh to God..57

Chapter 7: Enmity with God..63

Chapter 8: But He Giveth More Grace 71

Chapter 9: God Resisteth the Proud..81

Chapter 10: God Giveth Grace unto the Humble 91

2 Chronicles 7:12-14

Chapter 11: If My People 101

Chapter 12: If I Send Pestilence among My People 111

Chapter 13: If My People Shall Humble Themselves 119

Chapter 14: Then Will I Hear from Heaven 127

Psalm 51:1-3, 16-17

Chapter 15: The Sacrifices of God Are a Broken Spirit 137

Chapter 16: A Broken and A Contrite Heart 145

Chapter 17: For I Acknowledge My Transgressions 153

Chapter 18: Create in Me a Clean Heart 161

Chapter 19: Then Will I Teach Transgressors 169

Isaiah 66:1-2, 5

Chapter 20: To This Man Will I Look 177

Chapter 21: To Him that Is of a Contrite Spirit 185

Chapter 22: To Him that Trembleth at My Word 191

Chapter 23: Humble Yourselves Therefore 199

Preface

Revival NOW!

This preface is not presented in the common manner of our times – concerning the reasons that this book has been written. Rather, I believe that the Lord has directed me simply to present a message entitled "Revival NOW!" that the Holy Spirit of God developed within my heart from Isaiah 57:15. I had the privilege by God's mercy and grace to preach this message for the first time at a local church conference for revival on January 12, 2010. Because this message was originally prepared and presented before the book was in mind, some of the truths of this message may be repeated and reexamined in later chapters.

Isaiah 57:15 reads, ***"Thus saith the high and lofty One that inhabiteth eternity, whose name is Holy; I dwell in the high and holy place, with him also that is of a contrite and humble spirit, to revive the spirit of the humble, and to revive the heart of the contrite ones."***

Brethren, there are two great elements in this cause for "revival now." Each one of these two elements is communicated in the two separate words of the title. First, in the word "revival" is communicated the need *for the knowledge of the truth* (or, doctrine) of Biblical revival. Second, in the word "now" is communicated the need *for the experience of the life* of Biblical revival. Even so, brethren, a conference for the cause of revival is intended *to proclaim the truth* of revival and *to motivate us unto the life* of revival. In this message the Lord our God has directed that we consider six foundational principles concerning both the truth and life of Biblical revival.

Biblical Revival Is a Matter for God's People.

Isaiah 57:15 speaks concerning God's work of revival. Verse 14 reveals the people for whom this divine work of revival is made available. There we read, *"And shall say, Cast ye up, cast ye up, prepare the way, take up the stumblingblock out of the way of my people."* Spiritual revival refers to a return by *God's people* unto abundant spiritual life. It refers to a return by *God's people* unto Spirit-filled, spiritually fruitful and victorious Christian living. Such spiritual revival is not available to the lost souls of this world. They cannot return to abundant spiritual life because they are spiritually *"dead in trespasses and sins."* (Ephesians 2:1) Spiritually lost souls do not need spiritual revival; they need spiritual regeneration (new birth). They need to be spiritually born again.

However, we who are God's people through faith in the Lord Jesus Christ for salvation often need spiritual revival. We often need a return to abundant Christian living. In the closing portion of John 10:10, our Lord Jesus Christ declared, *"I am come that they might have life, and that they might have it more abundantly."* In His work of eternal salvation, our Lord came, not only to give us spiritual regeneration life, not only to give us newness of spiritual life, but also to give us that very regeneration life in a way of abundant spiritual living. Yet far too often we who are God's people go away backward from this abundance of spiritual living into the ways of sin. At such times we do not lose our spiritual regeneration life; but we do lose our spiritually abundant living, our Spirit-filled, spiritually fruitful and victorious Christian living. This is when we who are God's people need Biblical revival. Biblical revival is a matter for *God's people*.

Biblical Revival Is a Matter of Spiritual Fellowship.

The message that the Lord our God, *"the high and lofty One that inhabiteth eternity, whose name is Holy,"* delivers in Isaiah 57:15 begins with the phrase, *"I dwell in the high and holy place, with him . . ."* This phrase indicates that Biblical revival involves our Lord's *dwelling with* us. This refers to our Lord's *fellowship* with us and our *fellowship* with Him. In addition, this phrase indicates that Biblical revival involves our Lord's dwelling with us in the fellowship of His *"high and holy place."* This refers to our Lord's *spiritual* fellowship with us and our *spiritual* fellowship with Him.

Biblical revival is not about emotional excitement, or religious experience, or church expansion, or ministry exertion, or Biblical expounding, or even witnessing expression. It is possible to have any or all of these things in outward activity without having personal fellowship with the Lord our God.

Now, certainly if we are walking in personal fellowship with our Lord, if we are walking in revived, abundant Christian living, then we will know *"**joy unspeakable and full of glory**"* and *"**the peace of God, which passeth all understanding.**"* (1 Peter 1:8 & Philippians 4:7) Then certainly we will be more faithful in prayer, Bible study, ministry, and witnessing; and then certainly we will experience more spiritual effectiveness in our daily walk and ministry activities. Yet all of these things are the *fruit* of Biblical revival. The *foundation* for all of these fruits is our spiritual fellowship with the Lord. This spiritual fellowship is the very *essence* of Biblical revival. Biblical revival is a matter of *spiritual fellowship*.

Biblical Revival Is a Matter of Humble Repentance.

In Isaiah 57:15 the message of our Lord continues, *"**I dwell in the high and holy place, with him also that is of a contrite and humble spirit, to revive the spirit of the humble, and to revive the heart of the contrite ones.**"* Yet over what is this contrite and humble spirit necessary? Our Lord's continuing message in verses 16-17 reveals the answer, saying, *"**For I will not contend for ever, neither will I be always wroth: for the spirit should fail before me, and the souls which I have made. For the iniquity of his covetousness was I wroth, and smote him: I hid me, and was wroth, and he went on frowardly in the way of his heart.**"*

Brethren, the issue is an issue of sin and iniquity in our lives. Biblical revival is necessary in our lives whenever we turn aside from our spiritual fellowship with our Lord in order to walk in the ways of sin. Whenever we walk away from our Lord's fellowship into the ways of sin, we must come to a broken and contrite heart of confession and repentance in order to be spiritually revived and raised up again by the gracious hand of our Lord unto the high and holy place of His fellowship.

Even so, in the New Testament passage of James 4:4, the rebuke is given to the people of God unto whom James was writing, "***Ye adulterers and adulteresses, know ye not that the friendship of the world is enmity with God? Whosoever therefore will be a friend of the world is the enemy of God.***" Then in verses 8-10 the solution to this sinfulness and broken fellowship with the Lord is given, "***Draw nigh to God, and he will draw nigh to you.*** [How then do we draw nigh to God for spiritual fellowship when we are in the darkness of our sin?] *Cleanse your hands, ye sinners; and purify your hearts, ye double minded. Be afflicted, and mourn, and weep* [that is – with a broken and contrite heart over your sin]*: let your laughter be turned to mourning, and your joy to heaviness* [over your sin]*. Humble yourselves in the sight of the Lord* [over your sin]*, and he shall lift you up* [to the high and holy place of His blessed fellowship]." Biblical revival is matter of *humble repentance*.

Biblical Revival Is a Matter of Personal Decision.

In Isaiah 57:15 the message of our Lord is delivered unto individuals – "***I dwell in the high and holy place, with him also that is of a contrite and humble spirit.***" The word "him" is a singular pronoun. It focuses upon each one of us as an *individual*. *Each* one of us as an *individual* must come to humble, broken-hearted repentance of *our own* sin against the Lord our God; and *each* one of us as an *individual* must walk in *personal* fellowship with the Lord our God.

Just as it is true that each one of us must place his or her personal heart-trust in God the Son, the Lord Jesus Christ, for eternal salvation and spiritual regeneration; even so it is also true that each one of us must come to broken-hearted repentance of sin before the Lord for spiritual revival and restoration to the Lord's fellowship. Certainly a Biblical revival may sweep through a church or a community and may encompass a multitude of individuals. Yet it encompasses that multitude of individuals on an *individual* basis.

Furthermore, Biblical revival does not have to encompass a multitude within a church or community in order for one individual to experience a true, spiritual revival. Just as it is true in the case of eternal salvation and spiritual regeneration; even so it is also true in the case of spiritual revival. If *just one* individual out of a multitude comes to heart-trust in Christ for salvation, then God's gift of eternal salvation and spiritual regeneration *has indeed come* to that individual. In like manner, if *just one* individual believer out of a multitude comes to broken-hearted repentance over sin, then God's gift of spiritual revival and restored fellowship *has indeed come* to that individual. Biblical revival is a matter of *personal decision*.

Biblical Revival Is a Matter of Daily Walk.

In Isaiah 57:15 the message of our Lord begins, "*I dwell in the high and holy place, with him . . .*" Here our Lord speaks of *dwelling* in fellowship with us. Now, this word "dwell" refers to something that is a daily matter. We may *visit* certain places upon *occasion*, but we *dwell* at a certain place on a *daily* basis. Even so, our Lord does not intend that we might simply visit the high and holy place of His fellowship upon occasion. Rather, our Lord intends that we would dwell in the high and holy place of His fellowship with him each and every day. Yea, in Luke 9:23 our Lord calls for us to deny ourselves, to take up our cross *daily*, and to follow in spiritual fellowship with Him.

Biblical revival is a matter of daily walk, and this leads to three very important applications. First, this means that we can indeed experience the walk of Biblical revival *now*, on this *very* day, at this *very* time. If we will meet the requirement of our Lord, we will know Biblical revival in our lives *NOW*.

Furthermore, this means that we may experience the walk of Biblical revival today, yet may depart from that walk of Biblical revival tomorrow. Biblical revival is *not* an everlasting experience; it is a daily, step-by-step *walk*. As we have learned, the essence of Biblical revival is spiritual fellowship with our Lord. Yet *any sin* of attitude, word, or action will *break* that fellowship with our Lord and will *remove* us from the path of spiritually abundant living. When we are walking in the spiritual darkness of sin, *broken-hearted repentance* will *return us* to the path of spiritual revival and fellowship with our Lord. Yet when we are walking in the spiritual light of fellowship with our Lord, *any sin* of *any kind* will *remove us* from the path of spiritual revival and fellowship with our Lord.

Finally, this means that we must *purposefully choose* each new day and each moment of each day to walk in spiritual fellowship with our Lord. In addition, each sin that we commit in attitude, word, or action, we must quickly confess with broken-hearted repentance in order that we may quickly return to spiritually revived, abundant Christian living. Biblical revival is a matter of *daily walk*.

Biblical Revival Is a Matter of God's Promise.

In Isaiah 57:15 our Lord proclaims His message in the form of a *promise* – "***I dwell in the high and holy place, with him also that is of a contrite and humble spirit, to revive the spirit of the humble, and to revive the heart of the contrite ones.***" In addition, in verses 18-19 our Lord gives the promise, "***I have seen his ways*** [that is – his sinful ways, as mentioned in verses 16-17], ***and will heal him: I will lead him also, and restore comforts unto him and to his mourners. I create the fruit of the lips; Peace, peace to him that is far off, and to him that is near, saith the LORD; and I will heal him.***"

Now, every promise of the Lord our God is absolutely certain; for our Lord cannot and will not ever be unfaithful to Himself or to His Word. Even so, this promise of revival is absolutely certain for us who are God's people. On the foundation of God's own Word of promise, we can experience Biblical revival in our individual lives *NOW*, if we will meet our Lord's requirement.

Yet, as is commonly true for most of our Lord's promises, there is indeed a requirement that we must meet. In the passage our Lord's promise is *only* made available to those who are of a *contrite* and *humble* spirit before Him. In like manner, James 4:6 declares the truth, "***But he giveth more grace. Wherefore he saith, God resisteth the proud, but giveth grace unto the humble;***" and verse 10 delivers the instruction and the promise, "***Humble yourselves in the sight of the Lord, and he shall lift you up.***"

Preface

To those among us who will be of a contrite and humble spirit, God's promise is certain – Revival NOW! On the other hand, to those who are of a wickedly stubborn and proud spirit, the warning is given in Isaiah 57:20-21, "***But the wicked are like the troubled sea, when it cannot rest, whose waters cast up mire and dirt. There is no peace, saith my God, to the wicked*** [that is – to those among God's people who refuse to be of a contrite and humble spirit before the Lord over their sinfulness]."

Isaiah 57:15-21

For thus saith the high and lofty One
that inhabiteth eternity, whose name is Holy;
I dwell in the high and holy place,
with him also that is of a contrite and humble spirit,
to revive the spirit of the humble,
and to revive the heart of the contrite ones.
For I will not contend for ever,
neither will I be always wroth:
for the spirit should fail before me,
and the souls which I have made.
For the iniquity of his covetousness was I wroth,
and smote him: I hid me, and was wroth,
and he went on frowardly in the way of his heart.
I have seen his ways, and will heal him:
I will lead him also,
and restore comforts unto him and to his mourners.
I create the fruit of the lips;
Peace, peace to him that is far off,
and to him that is near, saith the LORD;
and I will heal him.
But the wicked are like the troubled sea,
when it cannot rest, whose waters cast up mire and dirt.
There is no peace, saith my God, to the wicked.

Chapter One

------~*~------

Thus Saith the High and Lofty One

Revival! Is there any need for a true, spiritual revival in our time? Certainly as we observe the moral corruption of our society and the continuing movement away from the Lord our God and His Word of truth, we recognize that there is a great need for true, spiritual revival. Ungodliness and unrighteousness abound on every side. Resistance and rebellion against the truth of God's Word is a central characteristic of the times. Society as a whole professes itself to be wise, while it is determined to pursue the foolishness of all ungodliness and unrighteousness. It ever hardens its heart more and more against the Lord God and ever hastens after the vanity of its own wicked imaginations. It has set its love upon the ways of spiritual darkness and has turned its hatred against the ways of Biblical light. *"There is no fear of God before their eyes."* (Romans 3:18)

The society of our time has rejected the Lord God from its thoughts and has given itself over to a reprobate mindset. It is ***"filled with all unrighteousness, fornication, wickedness, covetousness, maliciousness."*** (Romans 1:29) It is ***"full of envy, murder, debate, malignity."*** (Romans 1:29) It is given over to the slanderers and backbiters, to the haters of God, to the despiteful, to the proud and boastful, to the inventors of evil things, to those who are disobedient unto parental authority, to those without discernment, to those who do not keep their word of promise, to those without natural affection, to the implacable and unmerciful. (Romans 1:29-31)

Yet as bad as this may be, the case is far worse. Spiritual and moral corruption has invaded and overtaken the hearts and lives of our Lord's own people as well. So many of the Lord's own people, of those who profess the Lord Jesus Christ as their personal Savior, have forsaken our Lord and His ways. So many have gone away backward into the ways of sinfulness. So many are choosing their own way, walking after the selfishness of their own sinful flesh. So many are loaded down with the iniquity of ungodly thoughts, attitudes, words, and actions. So many are given over to selfishness and worldliness, loving and pursuing **"the lust of the flesh, and the lust of the eyes, and the pride of life."** (1 John 2:16) So many have set their love and affection on the things of this world, rather than upon the Lord our God and His righteousness.

Even among those who maintain an external appearance of godliness, so many are walking in spiritual hypocrisy, denying the Spirit-filled power of true godliness. So many draw nigh unto the Lord with their mouth and do honor the Lord with their lips, but they have removed their hearts far from Him. (Isaiah 29:13) With their mouths they proclaim much love to the Lord their God, but their hearts are given over to selfishness and covetousness. (Ezekiel 33:31) They come to hear the message of God's Holy Word, outwardly expressing delight therein; but they go forth in spiritual self-deception, refusing to obey its precepts. They are *not* doers of the Word, but hearers *only*, deceiving themselves. (James 1:22)

So many among our Lord's own people have no interest in the sound doctrine of God's Word. They gather to themselves teachers who will comfort them in their selfish desires, rather than confront them for their sinful ways. The leaders that they follow after teach the falsehood of men's ideas, rather than the truth of God's Word; and they love to have it so. They turn their ears away from the piercing conviction of God's truth. They are dull of hearing. They are hard of heart. They will not be broken and contrite of heart. They will not be of a meek and humble spirit. They will not live a yielded and surrendered life. They will not deny themselves. Rather, they live unto themselves. They will not lose their own will for the Lord's sake. Rather, they sacrifice the Lord's will for their own sake. They are **"lovers of pleasures more than lovers of God."** (2 Timothy 3:4)

Revival! Certainly there is a great need, but is there any assurance that this need can be met? Is there any assurance that we might claim true, spiritual revival for our lives, our marriages, our homes, our churches, and our communities? Any assurance upon which we might establish the confidence of our faith must come from the truth of God's Word and from our Lord God of truth. Even so, in Isaiah 57:15 the Word of God presents the promise of the Lord our God, saying, *"For thus saith the high and lofty One that inhabiteth eternity, whose name is Holy; I dwell in the high and holy place, with him also that is of a contrite and humble spirit, to revive the spirit of the humble, and to revive the heart of the contrite ones."* The Lord our God Himself has promised us the gracious blessing of spiritual revival.

What a wonderful promise! *"To revive the spirit of the humble, and to revive the heart of the contrite ones."* What an instructive promise! *"I dwell in the high and holy place, with him also that is of a contrite and humble spirit."* What a powerful promise! *"For thus saith the high and lofty One that inhabiteth eternity, whose name is Holy."* Now, it is upon the power of this promise that we shall focus our attention throughout the remainder of this chapter. The power of any promise is directly related to the nature of the one who has made the promise. The Lord our God Himself made the promise of Isaiah 57:15, and the power of this promise is founded upon His nature. Yea, in the opening portion of this verse, our Lord presents three specific elements of His nature as the substantial foundation for this promise.

The High and Lofty One

As the One who is making this promise, the Lord our God first presents Himself as *"the high and lofty One."* Thereby He reveals the *authority* of His promise. He is "the most high God." He is "the LORD most high." In Isaiah 6:1 the prophet Isaiah gave description of Him, saying, *"In the year that king Uzziah died I saw also the Lord sitting upon a throne, high and lifted up, and his train filled the temple."* He is the Lord God, supreme above all and sovereign over all. He sits upon His throne in heaven as the great King over all the earth. In Psalm 113:4-6 the psalmist exclaimed,

"The LORD is high above all nations, and his glory above the heavens. Who is like unto the LORD our God, who dwelleth on high, who humbleth himself to behold the things that are in heaven, and in the earth!" He is infinitely glorious in majesty. He is almighty in power. He is absolute Lord of all creation. There is none like unto Him. He is the one true and living Lord God, and there is none else beside Him.

The Lord our God is "the high and lofty One," and this He is as a very part of His eternal nature. He did not earn this high and lofty position. He did not labor to acquire this high and lofty position. He did not steal this high and lofty position from another. He was not placed into this high and lofty position by another. He did not *become* the high and lofty One. He *is*, and *always has been*, and *always shall be*, the high and lofty One. Lucifer, the high angel, sought after that high and lofty position. He thought to remove the Lord God from His high and lofty place and to establish himself in the Lord God's place. Yet this only resulted in Lucifer's great downfall out of his high, angelic place in heaven. Isaiah 14:12-15 gives the report, ***"How art thou fallen from heaven, O Lucifer, son of the morning! How art thou cut down to the ground, which didst weaken the nations! For thou hast said in thine heart, I will ascend into heaven, I will exalt my throne above the stars of God: I will sit also upon the mount of the congregation, in the sides of the north: I will ascend above the heights of the clouds; I will be like the most High. Yet thou shalt be brought down to hell, to the sides of the pit."*** The Lord God alone is "the high and lofty One." There can be none else, and there is none that can remove Him or replace Him.

He is the all-supreme and all-sovereign Creator God of all the creation. ***"By the word of the LORD were the heavens made; and all the host of them by the breath of his mouth."*** (Psalm 33:6) ***"Let all the earth fear the LORD: let all the inhabitants of the world stand in awe of him. For he spake, and it was done; he commanded, and it stood fast."*** By the very power of His word, He created all things; and by the word of His almighty power, He now upholds all things. (Hebrews 11:3; 1:3) All things, ***"that are in heaven, and that are in earth, visible and invisible,"*** were created by Him and for Him. (Colossians 1:16) *"And he is before all things, and by him all things consist."* (Colossians 1:17) He has created all things, and for His pleasure they are and were created. (Revelation 4:11) Even so, it is upon this all-supreme power and this all-sovereign authority that our Lord has founded His promise of revival in Isaiah 57:15.

The Eternal One

Furthermore, as the One who is making this promise, the Lord our God presents Himself as the One *"that inhabiteth eternity."* Thereby He reveals the *faithfulness* of His promise. He is the eternal and everlasting God. He lives within eternity as if it were His home. Thus in Psalm 90:2 the man of God Moses lifted up praise to Him, saying, *"Before the mountains were brought forth, or ever thou hadst formed the earth and the world, even from everlasting to everlasting, thou art God."* The Lord our God is *"most high for evermore."* (Psalm 92:7) His throne is established of old; He is from everlasting. (Psalm 93:2) His kingdom *"is an everlasting kingdom,"* and His dominion *"endureth throughout all generations."* (Psalm 145:13) He is *"the King eternal."* (1 Timothy 1:17) He is eternal in power and Godhead. (Romans 1:20) *"But the LORD is the true God, he is the living God, and an everlasting king."* (Jeremiah 10:10) In addition, being the eternal God, He is also the unchanging God. He is *"the Father of lights, with whom is no variableness, neither shadow of turning."* (James 1:17) The eternal perfection of His nature is unchanging and unchangeable.

Even so, being the eternally perfect Lord God, He is our eternally faithful Lord God. Infinitely great is His faithfulness. Through the absolute perfection of His eternal nature, He will never allow His faithfulness to fail. Yea, in Psalm 90:2 Moses presented the truth that our eternal Lord God is *"from everlasting to everlasting"* as the very foundation for the assurance of verses 1 – *"Lord, thou hast been our dwelling place in all generations."* Because He is the eternal God, His faithful servants may always have full assurance of faith that He is their dwelling place. Again in Psalm 145:13 David presented the truth that our Lord God's kingdom is *"an everlasting kingdom"* as the foundation for the assurance of verse 14 – *"The LORD upholdeth all that fall, and raiseth up all those that be bowed down."* Because He is the eternal God, His faithful servants may always have full assurance of faith that He will uphold them. Thus Deuteronomy 33:27 specifically declares that *"the eternal God"* is the refuge of His own and that underneath them are His *"everlasting arms."* *"Hast thou not known? Hast thou not heard, that the everlasting God, the LORD, the Creator of the ends of the earth, fainteth not, neither is weary?"* (Isaiah 40:28) It is upon this eternal perfectness and this eternal faithfulness that our Lord has founded His promise of revival in Isaiah 57:15. *"For he is faithful that promised."* (Hebrews 10:23)

The Holy One

Finally, as the One who is making this promise, the Lord our God presents Himself as the One *"whose name is Holy."* Thereby He reveals the *righteousness* of His promise. His very name is Holy. This is not simply that His name is a holy name, but that we may know Him by the name, the Holy One. Just as we may know Him as the Eternal God, the Sovereign Lord, the Almighty Creator, the Most High, even so we may know Him as the Holy One. Just as these other names describe His very nature, even so this name also describes His nature. We may know Him as the Holy One because He is indeed One who is holy. The closing portion of 1 John 1:5 declares, *"God is light, and in him is no darkness at all."* This is the glory of His nature. He is *"glorious in holiness."* (Exodus 15:11) Thus the seraphim that are around His throne continually cry unto one another, *"Holy, holy, holy is the LORD of hosts: the whole earth is full of his glory."* (Isaiah 6:3)

Even so, in Psalm 145:17-21 David proclaimed, *"The LORD is righteous in all his ways, and holy in all his works. The LORD is nigh unto all them that call upon him, to all that call upon him in truth. He will fulfil the desire of them that fear him: he also will hear their cry, and will save them. The LORD preserveth all them that love him: but all the wicked will he destroy. My mouth shall speak the praise of the LORD: and let all flesh bless his holy name for ever and ever."* The promise of the Holy One shall be fulfilled in righteousness, holiness, goodness, and uprightness unto those that fear Him, love Him, and call upon Him in truth. *"**Holy and reverend is his name.**"* (Psalm 111:9) Holy and righteous is His promise.

*"**Bless the LORD, O my soul: and all that is within me, bless his holy name. Bless the LORD, O my soul, and forget not all his benefits: who forgiveth all thine iniquities; who healeth all thy diseases; who redeemeth thy life from destruction; who crowneth thee with lovingkindness and tender mercies; who satisfieth thy mouth with good things; so that thy youth is renewed like the eagle's.**"* (Psalm 103:1-5) Let us praise His great and terrible name; *"**for it is holy.**"* (Psalm 99:3) Let us exalt the Lord our God and worship at His feet; *"**for he is holy.**"* (Psalm 99:5) It is upon this holy name and this holy nature that our Lord has founded His promise of revival in Isaiah 57:15. *"**Our soul waiteth for the LORD: he is our help and our shield. For our heart shall rejoice in him, because we have trusted in his holy name. Let thy mercy, O LORD, be upon us, according as we hope in thee.**"* (Psalm 33:20-22)

Chapter Two

With Him of a Contrite and Humble Spirit

In the previous chapter the question was asked – Is there any need for a true, spiritual revival in our time? Considering the spiritual corruption both among the lost world and among God's own people, the answer was that there certainly is a great need. Then a second question was asked – Is there any assurance that this need can be met? Is there any assurance that true, spiritual revival is available to us? The answer rings back from the Lord our God Himself through His Holy Word in Isaiah 57:15, "*For thus saith the high and lofty One that inhabiteth eternity, whose name is Holy; I dwell in the high and holy place, with him also that is of a contrite and humble spirit, to revive the spirit of the humble, and to revive the heart of the contrite ones.*"

This divine promise is the unshakable ground for our assurance of faith. The need *can* be met – by the Lord our God. Revival *is* available to us – from the Lord our God. His very nature is the foundation for His promise. This is our assurance. The promise of revival is founded upon the authority of Him who is the high and lofty One, upon the faithfulness of Him who is the eternal One, upon the righteousness of Him who is the Holy One.

In the previous chapter we considered the opening portion of Isaiah 57:15, in which the Lord our God presented three great characteristics of His divine nature as the foundation for His message of promise. In this chapter we move to the remainder of the verse wherein our Lord delivers that message of promise. Our Lord begins this message with the two words, "I dwell." Every other part of this message is connected to these opening words and serves to modify the truth of these words.

Now, with these two opening words, "I dwell," our Lord directs our attention upon the presence of His abiding fellowship. Certainly from the teaching of God's Word, we understand that in His infinite nature the Lord our God is omnipresent (all-present). His infinite presence dwells in all places, including heaven, hell, and the uttermost parts of the earth, at the same time. (Psalm 139:7-10) In this sense, our Lord's infinite presence fills all the creation and dwells with every one of us, whether righteous or unrighteous. (Jeremiah 23:24; Acts 17:28) Yet in Isaiah 57:15 our Lord is not speaking concerning the infinite nature of His omnipresence, but concerning the blessed presence of His abiding fellowship. In this sense, all of the spiritual blessedness of our Lord's abiding fellowship may be intimately near with us or may be distantly far away from us, depending upon the righteousness of our walk before Him.

How then might we walk aright before our Lord in order that we might experience the spiritual blessedness of His abiding fellowship? Through His message of promise in Isaiah 57:15, our Lord gives answer with three truths concerning His abiding fellowship.

The Place of Abiding Fellowship

First, our Lord defines the place of His abiding fellowship, saying, ***"I dwell in the high and holy place."*** Certainly we would expect the high and lofty One, whose name is Holy, to dwell in the high and holy place. This truth is only natural and reasonable. Certainly we would expect our Lord's heavenly throne room, where He sits as the sovereign Lord God over all, to be supremely high in glory and absolutely holy in goodness.

Yet in the context of Isaiah 57:15, "the high and holy place" is not a reference to that distinct place called Heaven. Rather, it is a reference to that spiritual place where the Lord our God will walk in abiding fellowship with us, even while we walk upon this earth. It is a place in which our Lord will dwell *with us now* in this life – when we are "of a contrite and humble spirit." It is not the place of our heavenly home unto which we believers shall not attain until the appointed time of our death or of our Lord's return. Nor is it some specific physical location unto which we must physically travel. Rather, it is the spiritual place of our Lord's fellowship in which we may dwell with Him *now*, during each and every moment of our present, daily walk.

This "high and holy place" is the blessed, spiritual fellowship of our Lord. Certainly our future home in heaven will consist of eternally perfect and blessed fellowship with our Lord. Yet the grammatical structure of our Lord's message of promise indicates that the humble servants of the Lord may dwell *even now* with Him in this high and holy place. Thus it is the place to which the apostle John referred in 1 John 1:3-7. It is the place in which ***truly our fellowship is with the Father, and with his Son Jesus Christ.*** It is the place of walking in the spiritual light of righteousness and true holiness, even as the Lord our God dwells in the spiritual light. It is the place of walking with our Lord in the light and beauty of His holy fellowship. It is the place in which we may find fullness of joy in the Lord.

This "high and holy place" of our Lord's abiding fellowship is the place of spiritually abiding in our Lord Jesus Christ, and of His abiding in us. (John 15:4-5) It is the place of growing in grace and in the excellency of the knowledge of Christ Jesus our Lord. (2 Peter 3:18; Philippians 3:8) It is the place of beholding the glory of our Lord Jesus Christ, in which we are transformed into that same holy image ***"from glory to glory, even as by the Spirit of the Lord."*** (2 Corinthians 3:18) It is the place of following our Good Shepherd, the Lord Jesus Christ, as He leads us in the righteous paths by which we ought to go. (Psalm 23:1-3; Isaiah 48:17)

It is ***"the secret place of the most High"*** in which we ***"shall abide under the shadow of the Almighty."*** (Psalm 91:1) It is the place in which the Lord our God Himself, the most high God, the almighty God, the eternal God, is our refuge and strength in the time of trouble. (Psalm 46:1) It is the place in which He Himself is our help, and hope, and hiding place, to preserve us from trouble and to compass us about with songs of deliverance. (Psalm 32:7) It is the place in which He Himself will uphold us with the right hand of His righteousness. (Isaiah 41:10) It is the place in which our Lord has laid up His great goodness and marvelous kindness for them that humbly fear Him and trust in Him. (Psalm 31:19-21) It is the place in which His great goodness and everlasting mercy shall surely follow with us all the days of our lives. (Psalm 23:6)

It is the place in which, although our feet are planted firmly upon this earth, traveling through the troubles and tribulations of this life, our hearts may rise high above in blessed, abiding fellowship with our Lord. It is the place in which, although we may travel *"through the valley of the shadow of death,"* our hearts will not be afraid or dismayed, because He Himself is with us. (Psalm 23:4) It is the place in which His rod and His staff do comfort us. It is the place in which the perfect peace of God, which surpasses all human understanding, shall guard our hearts and minds from being troubled. (Philippians 4:7)

The Prerequisite for Abiding Fellowship

Yet the high and holy place of our Lord's abiding fellowship is not promised to all. Rather, it is promised *only* to those who meet the established requirement of the Lord our God. Even so, as He continues His message of promise in Isaiah 57:15, our Lord delivers the prerequisite for His abiding fellowship, saying, **"*I dwell in the high and holy place, with him also that is of a contrite and humble spirit.*"**

Now, the Lord our God dwells in the high and holy place by nature. As **"*the high and lofty One that inhabiteth eternity, whose name is Holy,*"** He dwells naturally and eternally in that high and holy place. Yet if we who are the servants of the Lord are to dwell with Him in the fellowship of the high and holy place, then *He* must raise us up to it. We do not dwell in the fellowship of this high and holy place by our own nature, and we cannot attain unto the fellowship of this high and holy place through our own ability. The Lord *alone* can lift us up to the fellowship of His high and holy place. If He will not lift us up thereto, then we will never enter therein.

Yet our Lord *has* graciously expressed His desire that we should join with Him in the high and holy place of His abiding fellowship. Indeed He dwells in the high and holy place by nature. Yet He has graciously declared His desire to dwell there *with us also*. He *has* graciously opened the way that we might have the privilege to dwell with Him in the high and holy place of His abiding fellow-ship. He *has* graciously made the promise to lift us up unto that high and holy place of abiding fellowship with Him – *if* we will be "of a contrite and humble spirit."

The Lord our God *alone* is THE most high God. The Lord our God *alone* is THE high and lofty One. He will not abide those who attempt to lift up themselves before Him. Those who exalt themselves He will make low. (Isaiah 2:10-17; Matthew 23:12) He will not abide those who walk with a lofty look, a boasting tongue, a proud spirit, and a haughty heart. A proud spirit is a hateful abomination in His sight. (Proverbs 6:16-17) He will "***bring down high looks.***" (Psalm 18:27) "***Surely he scorneth the*** [proud and haughty] ***scorners.***" (Proverbs 3:34) "***Every one that is proud in heart is an abomination to the LORD: though hand join in hand, he shall not be unpunished.***" (Proverbs 16:5) By His very nature the Lord our God "***resisteth the proud.***" (James 4:6)

On the other hand, by His very nature the Lord our God "***giveth grace unto the humble.***" (James 4:6) "***Though the LORD be high,***" yea, though He be THE high and lofty Lord God over all, "***yet hath he respect unto the lowly.***" (Psalm 138:6) The contrite and humble ones He will not despise. Rather, our Lord will lift up those of a contrite and humble spirit to dwell with Him in the high and holy place of His abiding fellowship. He will look with favor upon them. (Isaiah 66:2) He will take pleasure in them and will beautify them with salvation. (Psalm 149:4) He will be near unto them in fellowship to hear their cry in the time of trouble and to deliver them. (Psalm 34:17-19) He will guide them and teach them in His way. (Psalm 25:7) He will cause them to increase their joy in Him. (Isaiah 29:19) He will cause them to "***delight themselves in the abundance of peace.***" (Psalm 37:11) He will grant to them the gracious gift of spiritual revival. In Isaiah 57:15 He declared, "***I dwell in the high and holy place, with him also that is of a contrite and humble spirit, to revive the spirit of the humble, and to revive the heart of the contrite ones.***"

Yet in what manner must we be of a contrite and humble spirit in order to enter into our Lord's promise of abiding fellowship and spiritual revival? The answer is found in the further context of verses 16-17. There our Lord bore record concerning His people, saying, *"For I will not contend for ever, neither will I be always wroth: for the spirit should fail before me, and the souls which I have made. For the iniquity of his covetousness was I wroth, and smote him: I hid me, and was wroth, and he went on frowardly in the way of his heart."*

The issue is the iniquity of our hearts and lives. Yea, the issue is the iniquity of our selfishness, covetousness, and worldliness. For this iniquity our Lord's wrath is kindled against us, and His hand of chastening is stretched forth to smite us. For this iniquity our Lord hides the grace of His favor and help from us and stands in contention and resistance against us. Our iniquities separate between us and the Lord our God and hide His face from us so that He *will not* hear our cry for grace to help in our time of need. (Isaiah 59:2) Yet so often, even under such chastening from our Lord, we continue stubbornly and rebelliously in the way of our own sinful hearts. Thus day and night our Lord's hand of chastening also continues to be heavy upon us, grievously pressing us down until we will come unto a broken and contrite heart of repentance. (Psalm 32:4)

However, when we will come to the place of a contrite and humble spirit over the iniquity of our sins and transgressions against our Lord, then He will be *"faithful and just to forgive us our sins, and to cleanse us from all unrighteousness."* (1 John 1:9) This is the contrite and humble spirit for which our Lord is seeking. We must *humbly* acknowledge and confess the evil of our sin against the Lord. We must turn from our wicked ways with *broken-hearted* repentance. We must plead the loving kindness and tender mercy of the Lord as our *only* hope for forgiveness, cleansing, deliverance, and restoration. *"The sacrifices of God are a broken spirit: a broken and a contrite heart, O God, thou wilt not despise."* (Psalm 51:17) This is the contrite and humble spirit to which our Lord has made His promise.

The Promise in Abiding Fellowship

Even so, in Isaiah 57:15 our Lord declares the promise in His abiding fellowship, saying, "***I dwell in the high and holy place, with him also that is of a contrite and humble spirit, to revive the spirit of the humble, and to revive the heart of the contrite ones.***" This is a revival *promise* from the Lord our God to us who are His people. This promise is *absolutely sure* and *eternally certain*. The Lord our God *cannot* lie, and He *will not* be unfaithful to His word of promise. We *can* claim this promise with *full assurance* of faith. If we will be of a contrite and humble spirit before the Lord over our sin against Him, He *will* lift us up to the high and holy place of His abiding fellowship and *will* revive us again spiritually in that abiding fellowship.

He *will* revive "***the spirit of the humble***" and "***the heart of the contrite ones.***" He *will* remove His heavy hand of chastening from grievously pressing us down in misery, and *will* reach forth His open hand of blessing to lift us up unto the high and holy place of His abiding fellowship. He *will* wash us thoroughly from our iniquity, and *will* cleanse us from our sin. (Psalm 51:2) He *will* lift us up out of the horrible pit and miry clay of our sinful iniquities, which had taken hold upon us until our hearts were failing within us. (Psalm 40:1-2, 12) He *will* set our feet upon the rock of His high and holy fellowship, and *will* establish our goings in His good, and acceptable, and perfect will.

He *will* revive us again, and create in us a clean heart. (Psalm 51:10) He *will* revive us again, and renew a right spirit within us. He *will* revive us again, and restore unto us the joy of His salvation. He *will* revive us again, that we might rejoice in Him. (Psalm 85:6) He *will* revive us again, and heal our broken hearts. He *will* revive us again, and comfort our weary souls. He *will* revive us again, that we might grow in Him. He *will* revive us again, and fill us anew with the spiritual strength of His indwelling Holy Spirit. (Ephesians 3:16) He *will* revive us again, and grant unto us abundant, spiritual life. (John 10:10)

He *will* fill us with Himself, and we shall find our sufficiency of Him. (2 Corinthians 3:5) He *will* pour out His grace abundantly upon us, and we shall find His grace to be sufficient for all our need. (James 4:6; 2 Corinthians 12:9) The Lord our God *will* become the portion of our inheritance and of our cup. (Psalm 16:4) In Him our hearts *will* be glad, and our flesh *will* rest in hope. (Psalm 16:9) From Him we *will* learn the path of abundant life, and in His presence we *will* find fullness of joy. (Psalm 16:11)

Oh, what a blessed promise is this! Oh, what an instructive promise is this! Oh, how important then is this – that we be of a contrite and humble spirit before the Lord our God!

Chapter Three

To Revive the Spirit of the Humble

In Isaiah 57:15 the Lord our God, *"the high and lofty One that inhabiteth eternity, whose name is Holy,"* has proclaimed His promise of spiritual revival, saying, *"I dwell in the high and holy place, with him also that is of a contrite and humble spirit, to revive the spirit of the humble, and to revive the heart of the contrite ones."* This is a sure and certain promise from our Lord who cannot and will not be unfaithful to His Word. This is a blessed promise – *if* we will be of a contrite and humble spirit before our Lord. This is an instructive promise – that we *must* be of a contrite and humble spirit before our Lord. This is a powerful promise – to those who *will be* of a contrite and humble spirit before our Lord.

Yet what is involved in our Lord's promise of spiritual revival? The answer to this question is revealed in the further context of verses 16-21. In verse 15 our Lord proclaimed His promise of spiritual revival. Then in verses 16-21 He presented His explanation concerning the matter.

In verses 16-17 our Lord presented *the need for* spiritual revival, saying, *"For I will not contend for ever, neither will I be always wroth: for the spirit should fail before me, and the souls which I have made. For the iniquity of his covetousness was I wroth, and smote him: I hid me, and was wroth, and he went on frowardly in the way of his heart."* The need for spiritual revival arises when we enter into the iniquity of sin, and when we stubbornly refuse to repent of our sin, but rebelliously continue in our sinful ways. For this sinful iniquity and stubborn rebellion, our Lord's wrath is kindled against us. For this sinful iniquity and stubborn rebellion, our Lord's hand of chastening strikes heavily upon us. For this sinful iniquity and stubborn rebellion, our Lord's gracious fellowship and favor is hidden from us. For this sinful iniquity and stubborn rebellion, our Lord stands in contention and resistance against us. Because of our sinful iniquity and stubborn rebellion, we need spiritual revival.

Then in verses 18-19 our Lord presented *the nature of* spiritual revival, saying, "***I have seen his ways, and will heal him: I will lead him also, and restore comforts unto him and to his mourners. I create the fruit of the lips; Peace, peace to him that is far off, and to him that is near, saith the LORD; and I will heal him.***" Herein our Lord reveals four great benefits that He will graciously bestow upon us who are His people through the gift of spiritual revival. These four benefits include – healing from the corruption of sin, leading in the way of righteousness, restoring to the comforts of fellowship, and upholding through the peace of God. These are the four great and gracious benefits that the Lord our God promises in this context for all of us who will be of a contrite and humble spirit before Him over our sinful iniquity and stubborn rebellion. In the remainder of this chapter, we shall examine the first of these four benefits more closely. Then in the next chapter we shall consider the latter three.

Finally, in verses 20-21 our Lord presented *the negation from* spiritual revival, saying, "***But the wicked are like the troubled sea, when it cannot rest, whose waters cast up mire and dirt. There is no peace, saith my God, to the wicked.***" This is our Lord's warning concerning our sinful iniquity and stubborn rebellion. If we will not be of a contrite and humble spirit before our Lord, then He will not grant to us His gracious gift of spiritual revival. If we stubbornly refuse to repent of our sinful ways and stubbornly rebel against our Lord's hand of chastening, then we will continue to suffer trouble under His chastening hand and will never find the comforts of His abiding fellowship. Then we will continue to walk in sinful corruption and will never find the place of cleansing or the path of righteousness. Then we will continue to be without spiritual rest and will never find the upholding of God's perfect peace.

Healing from the Corruption of Sin

In His promise of revival from Isaiah 57:15, our Lord promised *"to revive the spirit of the humble, and to revive the heart of the contrite ones."* This was not a reference to some physical revival of the physical body. Rather, this was a reference to a spiritual revival of the inner man, of the spirit and of the heart. What then is involved in such a spiritual revival? As we have previously noted, our Lord provides a four-fold answer in verses 18-19.

First, our Lord promises that He, in His gracious work of revival, will spiritually heal those of a contrite and humble spirit from the corrupttion of their sin. He declares in the opening portion of verse 18, *"I have seen his ways, and I will heal him."* Again He declares at the end of verse 19, *"And I will heal him."* Yet there is nothing in the context that would indicate a physical, health need. Our Lord does not indicate that He had seen the *physical weakness* of this one whom He would heal. Rather, our Lord indicates that He had seen the *spiritual ways* of this one whom He would heal. Previously in verse 17, He had reported these spiritual ways to be ways of sinful iniquity and stubborn frowardness. In this context the need for which our Lord grants His divine healing is not physical, but spiritual.

In the first chapter of the book of Isaiah, a foundational understanding is revealed for the Lord's entire message through His prophet. This foundational understanding concerned the spiritual condition of God's people at that time. In verses 2-4 the Lord proclaimed, *"Hear, O heavens, and give ear, O earth: for the LORD hath spoken, I have nourished and brought up children, and they have rebelled against me. The ox knoweth his owner, and the ass his master's crib: but Israel doth not know, my people doth not consider. Ah sinful nation, a people laden with iniquity, a seed of evildoers, children that are corrupters: they have forsaken the LORD, they have provoked the Holy One of Israel unto anger, they are gone away backward."*

God's own people had spiritually gone away backward from the Lord through sinful iniquity and stubborn rebellion. Thus our Lord gave the report in the closing portion of verse 5, saying, *"The whole head is sick, and the whole heart faint."* To this He added the report of verse 6, saying, "*From the sole of the foot even unto the head there is no soundness in it; but wounds, and bruises, and putrifying sores: they have not been closed, neither bound up, neither mollified with ointment.*" This was not a description of a physical problem, but of a spiritual problem. This was the description by the Lord Himself concerning the spiritual corruption by which their own iniquity and rebellion were consuming them. Even so, this same description is also true of us today when we give ourselves to sinful iniquity and stubborn rebellion against our Lord. In His sight we are spiritually sick and corrupted. In His sight there is no spiritual health in us. In His sight we are filled with spiritual wounds, and bruises, and putrefying sores.

From this spiritual corruption we need spiritual healing, and this is just what our Lord promises in His gracious work of revival to those who will be of a contrite and humble spirit over their sin. In the opening portion of Jeremiah 3:22, He delivers His call and His promise, saying, "*Return, ye backsliding children, and I will heal your backslidings.*" Again our Lord delivers His call to His backslidden people in Hosea 14:1, saying, "*O Israel, return unto the LORD thy God; for thou hast fallen by thine iniquity.*" Then He adds His promise in verse 4, saying, "*I will heal their backsliding, I will love them freely: for mine anger is turned away from him.*"

Yet what does it mean for our Lord to heal us spiritually?

> **Forgiveness and Cleansing**

For our Lord to heal us spiritually means that He will *forgive us and cleanse us from all our unrighteousness and iniquity.* In Jeremiah 33:2-3 our Lord proclaimed concerning His people Israel and concerning the city of Jerusalem, "*Thus saith the LORD the maker thereof, the LORD that formed it, to establish it; the LORD is his name; Call unto me, and I will answer thee, and shew thee great and mighty things, which thou knowest not.*" Then in verses 4-5 the Lord gave report concerning His chastening in His anger and in His fury upon His people for their wickedness and rebellion against Him. Yea, He determined to deliver His people over into the hand of the Chaldeans that they might be defeated, destroyed, and driven into captivity.

Yet in verses 6-8 our Lord revealed the great and mighty thing that He intended to do for His chastened people. There He gave promise, saying, *"Behold, I will bring it health and cure, and I will cure them, and will reveal unto them the abundance of peace and truth. And I will cause the captivity of Judah and the captivity of Israel to return, and will build them, as at the first. And I will cleanse them from all their iniquity, whereby they have sinned against me; and I will pardon all their iniquities, whereby they have sinned, and whereby they have transgressed against me."* This was our Lord's promise of spiritual healing for His people. He would remove the chastening of their captivity, and He would cleanse them and forgive them from all their iniquity. Even so, the promise of God's Word is given to us in 1 John 1:9, *"If we confess our sins* [with a contrite and humble spirit]*, he is faithful and just to forgive us our sins, and to cleanse us from all unrighteousness."*

Understanding this very principle, the man of God David, in his great prayer of broken-hearted confession and repentance, lifted up his request unto the Lord in Psalm 51:1-2, saying, *"Have mercy upon me, O God, according to thy lovingkindness: according unto the multitude of thy tender mercies blot out my transgressions. Wash me throughly from mine iniquity, and cleanse me from my sin."* Again he made request in verse 7, saying, *"Purge me with hyssop, and I shall be clean: wash me, and I shall be whiter than snow."* Yet again he made request in verse 9, saying, *"Hide thy face from my sins, and blot out all mine iniquities."*

> **Mercy and Deliverance**

Furthermore, for our Lord to heal us spiritually means that He will *remove His chastening hand from us and replace it with His merciful hand.* In Hosea 14:4 our Lord gave promise, saying, *"I will heal their backsliding, I will love them freely: for mine anger is turned away from him."* In His work of spiritual healing, our Lord turns away the anger of His chastening from us and pours out freely the love of His mercy upon us. Understanding this principle, the man of God David lifted up his prayer unto the Lord in Psalm 6:1-4, saying, *"O LORD, rebuke me not in thine anger, neither chasten me in thy hot displeasure. Have mercy upon me, O LORD; for I am weak: O LORD, heal me; for my bones are vexed. My soul is also sore vexed: but thou, O LORD, how long? Return, O LORD, deliver my soul: oh save me for thy mercies' sake."*

Under the anger and hot displeasure of the Lord's rebuke and chastening, David had been made weak unto his very bones, yea, unto the very depth of his inner man. Thus he prayed that the Lord might grant him spiritual healing. David prayed that the Lord might remove from him the anger and hot displeasure of His chastening hand, and that He might open unto him the help and blessed deliverance of His merciful hand. In His work of spiritual healing, our Lord does not simply remove His hand of chastening. He also reaches forth His hand of mercy to bind up and to heal the very wounds that He inflicted upon us through His chastening hand. Even so, the call and the promise is given in Hosea 6:1, *"Come, and let us return unto the LORD: for he hath torn, and he will heal us; he hath smitten, and he will bind us up."*

➢ **Fellowship and Fruitfulness**

Finally, for our Lord to heal us spiritually means that He will *restore us to spiritual fellowship with Him and spiritual fruitfulness through Him*. In Hosea 6:1-3 the truth concerning our Lord's work of spiritual healing continues, saying, *"Come, and let us return unto the LORD: for he hath torn, and he will heal us; he hath smitten, and he will bind us up. After two days will he revive us: in the third day he will raise us up, and we shall live in his sight. Then shall we know, if we follow on to know the LORD: his going forth is prepared as the morning; and he shall come unto us as the rain, as the latter and former rain unto the earth."* In His revival work of spiritual healing, our Lord not only binds up the wounds that He inflicted through His chastening, but also lifts us up to "live in His sight." Yea, He lifts us up to live and walk in the presence of His fellowship and favor.

Then we shall come to know the blessedness of spiritual fellowship with our Lord and spiritual revival from our Lord, if we continue to follow on with Him in our daily walk. Then we shall grow to know our Lord Himself more and more intimately in loving fellowship.

Then He shall create within us a clean heart and renew within us a right spirit. (Psalm 51:10) Then He shall surely go forth in fellowship with us each new day, and in His fellowship He Himself shall be unto us as the rain is unto the earth, producing growth and fruitfulness. If we will be of a contrite and humble spirit before Him over our sin, He will forgive us and cleanse us of all our iniquity; He will remove His chastening hand from us and open His merciful hand toward us; and He will immediately lift us up and restore us to the high and holy place of fellowship with Him. Then, if we will continue to follow on with Him in that fellowship, He Himself will work upon us, in us, and through us to bring forth spiritual fruit for the glory of His name.

Concerning His people Israel, our Lord declared in Hosea 14:4-7, *"I will heal their backsliding, I will love them freely: for mine anger is turned away from him. I will be as the dew unto Israel: he shall grow as the lily, and cast forth his roots as Lebanon. His branches shall spread, and his beauty shall be as the olive tree, and his smell as Lebanon. They that dwell under his shadow shall return; they shall revive as the corn, and grow as the vine: the scent thereof shall be as the wine of Lebanon."* In His revival work of spiritual healing, He would be as the dew unto His people, causing them to grow abundantly in beauty and in fruitfulness.

In like manner, our Lord Jesus Christ gave instruction and promise unto us in John 15:4-5, saying, *"Abide in me, and I in you. As the branch cannot bear fruit of itself, except it abide in the vine; no more can ye, except ye abide in me. I am the vine, ye are the branches: he that abideth in me, and I in him, the same bringeth forth much fruit: for without me ye can do nothing."* Also in Colossians 1:9-10 the apostle Paul expressed his burden of prayer for the believers at Colossi, saying, *"For this cause we also, since the day we heard it, do not cease to pray for you, and to desire that ye might be filled with the knowledge of his will in all wisdom and spiritual understanding; that ye might walk worthy of the Lord unto all pleasing, being fruitful in every good work, and increasing in the knowledge of God."*

Brethren, this is our Lord's promised work of spiritual revival. This is our Lord's promised work of spiritual healing. If we will bow before Him with a contrite and humble spirit, He will lift us up unto His fellowship and favor; and if we will abide in His fellowship and favor, He will cause us to be "fruitful in every good work" and to be "increasing in the knowledge of God."

Chapter Four

To Revive the Heart of the Contrite

As we noted in the previous chapter, in Isaiah 57:18-19 our Lord reveals four great benefits that He will graciously bestow upon us who are His people through the gift of spiritual revival. In verse 15 our Lord delivers His promise to revive the heart and spirit of those who will be of a contrite and humble spirit before Him. Then in verses 18-19 our Lord reveals the benefits that are included in His work of spiritual revival, saying, *"I have seen his ways, and will heal him: I will lead him also, and restore comforts unto him and to his mourners. I create the fruit of the lips; Peace, peace to him that is far off, and to him that is near, saith the LORD; and I will heal him."*

Already in the previous chapter, we have considered the first of these four revival benefits – the benefit of healing from the corruption of sin. In this chapter we shall consider the remaining three revival benefits – the benefits of leading in the way of righteousness, of restoring to the comforts of fellowship, and of upholding through the peace of God.

Leading in the Way of Righteousness

Our Lord promises that He, in His gracious work of revival, will spiritually lead those of a contrite and humble spirit in the way of righteousness. He declares in the opening portion of verse 18, *"I have seen his ways, and I will heal him: I will lead him also."* In

His gracious work of revival, our Lord not only grants us spiritual healing from the corruption of our past sins, but also provides us with personal guidance in the way of present righteousness. He not only delivers us out of the horrible pit and miry clay of our iniquities, but He also sets our feet upon a rock and establishes our goings through His personal direction. (Psalm 40:2)

If, with a contrite and humble spirit, we will return from our sinful wanderings unto the Lord as our Shepherd, He will restore our soul through His work of spiritual healing. Then if, with a contrite and humble spirit, we will continue to follow after our Lord as our Shepherd, He will lead us *"in the paths of righteousness for his name's sake."* (Psalm 23:3) If, with a contrite and humble spirit, we will confess our spiritual foolishness and sinful offense against the Lord and will continually draw near unto the Lord, He will lift us up by His almighty hand and will lead us with His all-wise counsel. (Psalm 73:21-24)

If, with a contrite and humble spirit, we will repent of our sinful iniquity, turn again unto the Lord, trust also in the Lord, wait continually on the Lord, and walk in the fear of the Lord, He will forgive all our sins, deliver us from our corruption, reveal unto us His ways, teach unto us His paths, and lead us in His truth. (Psalm 25) **"Good and upright is the LORD: therefore will he teach sinners in the way."** (Psalm 25:8) This is His gracious work of spiritual revival. This is His principle and promise of revival – **"The meek** [those of a contrite and humble spirit] **will he guide in judgment: and the meek** [those of a contrite and humble spirit] **will he teach his way."** (Psalm 25:9) This He will do according to His tender mercies and loving kindnesses for the glory of His own name and goodness.

If, with a contrite and humble spirit, we will acknowledge and confess our transgressions against the Lord, He will forgive the iniquity of our sin. (Psalm 32:5) Then if, with a contrite and humble spirit, we will continue to submit ourselves unto His lordship authority, He will instruct and teach us in the way which we should go. (Psalm 32:8) Yea, He will guide us with the loving kindness of His eye. If, with a contrite and humble spirit, we will trust in the Lord with all our heart and acknowledge His lordship in all our ways, He will direct our paths.

(Proverbs 3:5-6) He will cause us to know the way wherein we should walk. (Psalm 143:8) He will teach us to do His righteous will, to do that which is pleasing and acceptable in His sight. (Psalm 143:10) He will lead us into the land of uprightness.

He will lead us in His own righteousness. (Psalm 5:8) He will make His way of righteousness straight and clear before our face so that we might not turn aside to the right hand or to the left. He will hold up our goings in His own path of righteousness, so that our footsteps might not slip again into the horrible pit and miry clay of sin. (Psalm 17:5) He will order our steps in His Word, so that no iniquity might have dominion over us. (Psalm 119:133) He will ever order our steps and delight in our way, so that although we might fall to temptation, He is ever present to convict us, correct us, cleanse us, restore us, revive us, and reestablish us through the upholding of His hand. (Psalm 37:23-24)

When our heart is overwhelmed within us, He will lead us to the rock that is higher than we are. (Psalm 61:2) At the attack of our adversary the devil, He Himself will be our spiritual shelter and strong tower. (Psalm 61:3) If, with a contrite and humble spirit, we will set our trust in Him, He Himself will be our rock and our fortress. (Psalm 31:3) For His name's sake, He will lead us and guide us, so that we might be delivered from the wiles of our adversary the devil, the lures of this spiritually dark world, the desires of our sinful flesh, and the discouragements of our hateful persecutors.

Therefore, with a contrite and humble spirit, we must join with the man of God David in lifting up the prayer of Psalm 139:23-24 unto the Lord daily, saying, **"Search me, O God, and know my heart: try me, and know my thoughts: and see if there be any wicked way** [any way that offends and grieves the Lord] **in me, and lead me in the way everlasting."**

Restoring to the Comforts of Fellowship

Furthermore, our Lord promises that He, in His gracious work of revival, will spiritually restore those of a contrite and humble spirit unto the comforts of His fellowship. He declares in the closing portion of

Isaiah 57:18, "*I will lead him also, and restore comforts unto him and to his mourners.*" For those who will be of a contrite and humble spirit over their sinfulness, our Lord will turn the mourning of their sin's corruption and chastening to the joy of His fellowship and favor. This is our Lord's promise – "*Blessed are they that mourn: for they shall be comforted.*" (Matthew 5:4) If we will mourn with a contrite and humble spirit over our sin, our Lord will bless us with His comfort. He will restore unto us the joy of our salvation. (Psalm 51:12) Through His comforting work, He will fill us with joy and rejoicing in Him.

In Isaiah 12:1-3 God's Word gives promise concerning a great, future revival of the chosen people Israel, saying, "*And in that day thou shalt say, O LORD, I will praise thee: though thou wast angry with me, thine anger is turned away, and thou comfortedst me. Behold, God is my salvation; I will trust, and not be afraid: for the LORD JEHOVAH is my strength and my song; he also is become my salvation. Therefore with joy shall ye draw water out of the wells of salvation.*" Even so, the principle stands true for any of us who enter through a contrite and humble spirit into our Lord's promise of spiritual revival. The anger of His chastening hand will be turned away from us, and the blessing of His comforting hand will be set upon us. Then we will know the comforts of the Lord Jehovah as our strength, our song, and our salvation. Then we "shall draw water out of the wells of salvation." Yea, then we shall experience the ever-flowing, spiritual abundance of our newness of life in Christ.

Thus our Lord proclaimed in Isaiah 40:1-2, "*Comfort ye, comfort ye my people, saith your God. Speak ye comfortably to Jerusalem, and cry unto her, that her warfare is accomplished, that her iniquity is pardoned: for she hath received of the LORD'S hand double for all her sins.*" This was the ground for comfort from the Lord unto His people. The warfare of their chastening was complete, and the iniquity of their sin was pardoned. Even so, this remains the ground for comfort unto us who are God's people today. When we return unto our Lord with a contrite and humble spirit over our sin, He removes His chastening from us, forgives the iniquity of our sin, and proclaims His comfort to us.

Yet this is only the ground for our comfort. What is the manner in which this comfort is bestowed? Isaiah 40:9-11 reveals the answer, saying, *"O Zion, that bringest good tidings, get thee up into the high mountain; O Jerusalem, that bringest good tidings, lift up thy voice with strength; lift it up, be not afraid; say unto the cities of Judah, Behold your God! Behold, the Lord GOD will come with strong hand, and his arm shall rule for him: behold, his reward is with him, and his work before him. He shall feed his flock like a shepherd: he shall gather the lambs with his arm, and carry them in his bosom, and shall gently lead those that are with young."* Like a good, loving Shepherd, our Lord will feed us and care for us. Like a good, loving Shepherd, He will gather us to Himself in fellowship and will carry us in His bosom with favor. Like a good, loving Shepherd, He will lead us gently unto the place of rest and refreshing.

In addition, Isaiah 40:28-31 reveals the answer, saying, *"Hast thou not known? Hast thou not heard, that the everlasting God, the LORD, the Creator of the ends of the earth, fainteth not, neither is weary? There is no searching of his understanding. He giveth power to the faint; and to them that have no might he increaseth strength. Even the youths shall faint and be weary, and the young men shall utterly fall: but they that wait upon the LORD shall renew their strength; they shall mount up with wings as eagles; they shall run, and not be weary; and they shall walk, and not faint."* If, with a contrite and humble spirit, we will depend and wait upon the Lord, He, through His comforting work, will give spiritual power unto us when we are faint and weak. He will renew our spiritual strength so that we might rise above our troubles and might continue forward in His will without becoming wearied or discouraged in well doing.

Then we shall intimately know God our heavenly Father as *"the Father of mercies, and the God of all comfort; who comforteth us in all our tribulation, that we may be able to comfort them which are in any trouble, by the comfort wherewith we ourselves are comforted of God."* (2 Corinthians 1:3-4) Yea, though we may be called to the deepest, darkest trouble of walking *"through the valley of the shadow of death,"* our hearts shall be without any fear of evil;

for the Lord our God will be with us, and His rod and His staff will comfort us. (Psalm 23:4) His merciful kindness will be for our comfort and joy. (Psalm 119:76)

This is the certain principle of spiritual revival, even as the prayer of Psalm 85:6 reveals, saying, *"**Wilt thou not revive us again: that thy people may rejoice in thee?**"* When the Lord our God grants the gift of spiritual revival unto us who are of a contrite and humble spirit, He restores us unto the comforts and joy of His fellowship. Then we shall find that the Lord our God Himself is our exceeding joy. Then, as we abide in fellowship with Him, His joy shall remain in us; and our joy shall be made full. (John 15:11) Then, through faith in Him and fellowship with Him, we shall *"**rejoice with joy unspeakable and full of glory.**"* (1 Peter 1:8)

Upholding through the Peace of God

Finally, our Lord promises that He, in His gracious work of revival, will spiritually uphold those of a contrite and humble spirit through His own peace. He declares in Isaiah 57:19, *"**I create the fruit of the lips; Peace, peace to him that is far off, and to him that is near, saith the LORD; and I will heal him.**"* Now, in our Lord's gracious work of revival, this gift of peace is granted in a two-fold manner, in which the first is foundational and the second flows from the first.

First and foundational, in the work of revival we receive the gift of peace *with* God. As we have already learned from verses 16-17, when we enter into sinful iniquity and stubborn rebellion against our Lord, His anger and wrath will be kindled against us. In righteous anger, He will hide His gracious fellowship and favor from us. In righteous anger, His hand of chastening will move against us and will be heavy upon us. In righteous anger, He will smite us and will contend with us. In righteous anger, the Lord our God will stand at enmity against us in our daily walk.

Yet if, with a contrite and humble spirit, we will repent of our sinful iniquity and will return unto the Lord our God, then He will remove His righteous anger and chastening hand from us and will return unto us in blessed fellowship and gracious favor. The Lord our God will no longer be standing at enmity and contention with us over our sin, but will now be standing at peace and fellowship with us by His grace. Even so, the contrite and humble prayer for revival is lifted up in Psalm 85:4-7 – *"Turn us, O God of our salvation, and cause thine anger toward us to cease. Wilt thou be angry with us for ever? Wilt thou draw out thine anger to all generations? Wilt thou not revive us again: that thy people may rejoice in thee? Shew us thy mercy, O LORD, and grant us thy salvation."* Then in verse 8 the assurance of our Lord's gracious response is expressed – *"I will hear what God the LORD will speak: for he will speak peace unto his people, and to his saints: but let them not turn again to folly."*

Second, in the work of revival we receive the gift of peace *from* God. As we walk at peace and in fellowship with the Lord our God, He will grant us the gift of His own perfect peace, so that we might know fullness of peace in Him even as we face the greatest tribulations of this life. In John 14:27 our Lord Jesus Christ declared, *"Peace I leave with you, my peace I give unto you: not as the world giveth, give I unto you. Let not your heart be troubled, neither let it be afraid."* Again in John 16:33 He declared, *"These things I have spoken unto you, that in me ye might have peace. In the world ye shall have tribulation: but be of good cheer; I have overcome the world."* This is not the kind of peace that this world gives through its various methods and means, a peace that is shallow and short-lived. Rather, this is the supernatural peace of the Lord our God Himself, a peace that surpasses all natural understanding and that shall keep our hearts and minds untroubled even in the midst of life's greatest troubles. (Philippians 4:7)

If, with a contrite and humble spirit, we will set our thoughts and our trust upon our Lord, then He will keep us in the place of perfect peace. In Isaiah 26:3-4 the promise and instruction is given, *"Thou wilt keep him in perfect peace, whose mind is stayed on thee: because he trusteth in thee. Trust ye in the LORD for ever: for in the LORD JEHOVAH is everlasting strength."* If, with a contrite and humble spirit, we will submit ourselves to the yoke of our Lord's fellowship and authority, to learn of Him and be directed by Him, then we shall find peace and rest unto our souls. In Matthew 11:20 our Lord Jesus Christ gave the instruction and promise, *"Take my yoke upon you, and learn of me; for I am meek and lowly in heart: and ye shall find rest unto your souls."*

If, with a contrite and humble spirit, we will love the Word of God, to learn its truth and wisdom with joy, to meditate in its principles and precepts all the day, and to follow its counsels and commandments in faithful obedience, then we shall know the great peace of God. Yea, then we shall experience the peace of God in our hearts as a continuously flowing river. In Psalm 119:165 the promise is given, *"Great peace have they which love thy law: and nothing shall offend them."* Again in Isaiah 48:17-18 the truth and promise is given, *"Thus saith the LORD, thy Redeemer, the Holy One of Israel; I am the LORD thy God which teacheth thee to profit, which leadeth thee by the way that thou shouldest go. O that thou hadst hearkened to my commandments! Then had thy peace been as a river, and thy righteousness as the waves of the sea."*

Chapter Five

No Peace, Saith My God, to the Wicked

In Isaiah 57:15 the Lord our God delivers His certain promise of spiritual revival unto all who will be of a contrite and humble spirit before Him over their sin. *"For thus saith the high and lofty One that inhabiteth eternity, whose name is Holy; I dwell in the high and holy place, with him also that is of a contrite and humble spirit, to revive the spirit of the humble, and to revive the heart of the contrite ones."*

Then in verses 18-19 our Lord reveals the four-fold blessing that He will grant through His work of revival unto those of a contrite and humble spirit. *"I have seen his ways, and will heal him: I will lead him also, and restore comforts unto him and to his mourners. I create the fruit of the lips; Peace, peace to him that is far off, and to him that is near, saith the LORD; and I will heal him."*

However, in verses 20-21 the Lord our God delivers a solemn and serious warning unto all who rebelliously refuse to repent of their sin with a contrite and humble spirit. *"But the wicked are like the troubled sea, when it cannot rest, whose waters cast up mire and dirt. There is no peace, saith my God, to the wicked."*

Now, in this context these wicked ones are not simply those who have gone away backward into sinful iniquity and stubborn rebellion, as opposed to those who have remained in righteousness and godliness. In fact, those of verses 18-19, to whom our Lord grants the four-fold blessings of His revival work, and these wicked ones of verses 20-21, from whom our Lord withholds these blessings, are *both* defined in verses 16-17 as those among God's people who have committed sinful iniquity and have walked frowardly in the stubborn rebellion of their own hearts.

So then, what makes the difference? Why does our Lord grant the blessings of His revival work to those of verses 18-19, but not to these "wicked" ones of verses 20-21? The answer is to be found in our Lord's certain promise of spiritual revival in verse 15 – "*I dwell in the high and holy place, with him also that is of a contrite and humble spirit, to revive the spirit of the humble, and to revive the heart of the contrite ones.*" *All* had engaged in sinful iniquity. *All* had continued in stubborn rebellion. Yet some have now come to the place of repentance with a contrite and humble spirit. Such are those of verses 18-19, to whom our Lord grants the blessings of spiritual revival.

On the other hand, some have continually refused to come unto the place of repentance with a contrite and humble spirit. These are the wicked ones of verses 20-21, from whom our Lord withholds the blessings of spiritual revival. They have yet refused to meet our Lord's prerequisite for spiritual revival and abiding fellowship. In this context, they are *not* defined as "the wicked" because they have gone away backward into sinful iniquity and stubborn rebellion. Rather, they are defined as "the wicked" because they willfully refuse to repent thereof with a contrite and humble spirit.

To these wicked ones, who so willfully refuse to repent with a contrite and humble spirit, our Lord delivers a three-fold warning in verses 20-21. This warning is delivered through the picture of a troubled sea.

Unrelieved Chastening

First, our Lord warns that His hand of chastening will continue heavy upon such unrepentant ones without relief. He proclaims in the opening portion of verse 20, "*But the wicked are like the troubled sea, when it cannot rest.*" Just as our Lord's hand troubles the sea during a time of storm, even so His hand of chastening will trouble their hearts and lives so that they cannot rest.

Certainly God our heavenly Father chastens us who are His own dear children when we walk in disobedience and sin. Hebrews 12:6 states, *"For whom the Lord loveth he chasteneth, and scourgeth every son whom he receiveth."* This He does in order to move us unto the contrite and humble spirit of repentance that we might be revived spiritually and might bring forth the fruit of righteousness. Yet, if we refuse to come unto the contrite and humble spirit of repentance, our Lord's hand of chastening and *scourging* will only become heavier and more severe.

In Psalm 32:3-4 David described such a time in his life, saying, *"When I kept silence, my bones waxed old through my roaring all the day long. For day and night thy hand was heavy upon me: my moisture is turned into the drought of summer. Selah."* When David "kept silence," stubbornly refusing to acknowledge, confess, and repent of his sin with a contrite and humble spirit, he was troubled in heart and life "all the day long." This was so because the Lord's hand of chastening was heavy upon him. This was so because the Lord's hand of chastening was troubling his heart and life so that he could not rest.

Again in Psalm 38:1-11 David described such a time of heavy chastening, saying, *"O Lord, rebuke me not in thy wrath: neither chasten me in thy hot displeasure. For thine arrows stick fast in me, and thy hand presseth me sore. There is no soundness in my flesh because of thine anger; neither is there any rest in my bones because of my sin. For mine iniquities are gone over mine head: as an heavy burden they are too heavy for me. My wounds stink and are corrupt because of my foolishness. I am troubled; I am bowed down greatly; I go mourning all the day long. For my loins are filled with a loathsome disease: and there is no soundness in my flesh. I am feeble and sore broken: I have roared by reason of the disquietness of my heart. Lord, all my desire is before thee; and my groaning is not hid from thee. My heart panteth, my strength faileth me: as for the light of mine eyes, it also is gone from me. My lovers and my friends stand aloof from my sore; and my kinsmen stand afar off."*

Yet again in Psalm 39:10-11 David expressed his burden of prayer, saying, "*Remove thy stroke away from me: I am consumed by the blow of thine hand. When thou with rebukes dost correct man for iniquity, thou makest his beauty to consume away like a moth: surely every man is vanity. Selah.*" In like manner, Moses declared in Psalm 90:7-8, "*For we are consumed by thine anger, and by thy wrath are we troubled. Thou hast set our iniquities before thee, our secret sins in the light of thy countenance.*"

Finally, in Lamentations 3:1-20 the prophet Jeremiah, as a representative of God's nation Israel, cried forth, "*I am the man that hath seen affliction by the rod of his wrath. He hath led me, and brought me into darkness, but not into light. Surely against me is he turned; he turneth his hand against me all the day. My flesh and my skin hath he made old; he hath broken my bones. He hath builded against me, and compassed me with gall and travail. He hath set me in dark places, as they that be dead of old. He hath hedged me about, that I cannot get out: he hath made my chain heavy. Also when I cry and shout, he shutteth out my prayer. He hath inclosed my ways with hewn stone, he hath made my paths crooked. He was unto me as a bear lying in wait, and as a lion in secret places. He hath turned aside my ways, and pulled me in pieces: he hath made me desolate. He hath bent his bow, and set me as a mark for the arrow. He hath caused the arrows of his quiver to enter into my reins. I was a derision to all my people; and their song all the day. He hath filled me with bitterness, he hath made me drunken with wormwood. He hath also broken my teeth with gravel stones, he hath covered me with ashes. And thou hast removed my soul far off from peace: I forgat prosperity. And I said, My strength and my hope is perished from the LORD: remembering mine affliction and my misery, the wormwood and the gall. My soul hath them still in remembrance, and is humbled in me.*"

Continual Corruption

Second, our Lord warns that the unrepentant ones will continually bring forth more spiritual corruption and will be consumed in and by that very corruption. In Isaiah 57:20 He continues His proclamation, saying, "*But the wicked are like the troubled sea, when it cannot rest, whose waters cast up mire and dirt.*" Just as a troubled sea spews forth mire and dirt with each wave, even so their hearts and lives will bring forth spiritual corruption with each step of their daily walk, whether in attitude, word, or action.

In Isaiah 1:5 our Lord confronted the character of His unrepentant people, saying, "*Why should ye be stricken any more? Ye will revolt more and more: the whole head is sick, and the whole heart faint.*" No matter how much He chastened them, they would not repent. Instead they rebelled *more and more* until the whole head was overcome with spiritual corruption, and the whole heart was consumed by spiritual corruption. If we choose this path of unrepentant rebellion, we will sell ourselves unto wickedness, will become the servants of corruption, and will ever increase unto more ungodliness. We will ever proceed from evil to evil and will weary ourselves to commit iniquity.

To those of us who continue on the path of unrepentant rebellion, Proverbs 5:22-23 gives the warning – "*His own iniquities shall take the wicked himself, and he shall be holden with the cords of his sins. He shall die without instruction; and in the greatness of his folly he shall go astray.*" We will be taken captive and held fast by our own sinful iniquities. We will end our life in spiritual destitution and devastation, having never come to correction of sin and instruction in righteousness. In the great spiritual folly of an unrepentant heart, we will continually go astray from the Lord our God, from His blessed fellowship, and from His righteous will. Our hearts and lives will become spiritually withered. (John 15:6) Our Christian walk will be spiritually devoured by our adversary the devil. (1 Peter 5:8)

This is the solemn warning of our Lord. "*Then when lust hath conceived, it bringeth forth sin: and sin, when it is finished, bringeth forth death.*" (James 1:15) "*Be not deceived; God is not mocked: for whatsoever a man soweth, that shall he also reap. For he that soweth to his flesh shall of the flesh reap corruption.*" (Galatians 6:7-8a) "*The backslider in heart shall be filled with his own ways.*" (Proverbs 14:14a) "*For that they hated knowledge, and did not choose the fear of the* LORD: *they would none of my counsel: they despised all my reproof. Therefore shall they eat of the fruit of their own way, and be filled with their own devices."* (Proverbs 1:29-31)

No Peace

Third and finally, our Lord warns that the unrepentant ones will never know His perfect peace of heart and mind. In Isaiah 57:21 our Lord proclaims, *"There is no peace, saith my God, to the wicked."* If we choose and continue on the path of unrepentant rebellion, we will not know joy in the Lord or the joy of the Lord. Indeed we might *"enjoy the pleasures of sin for a season"* (Hebrews 11:24), but we will not rejoice in the fellowship of our Lord *"with joy unspeakable and full of glory."* (1 Peter 1:8) We will lose the joy of our salvation and will never have it restored as long as we refuse to repent with a contrite and humble spirit. We might have our emotional hurts healed slightly by the false, fleeting peace of this world (Jeremiah 6:14 & 8:11); but we will never know *"the peace of God, which passeth all understanding,"* keeping and guarding our hearts and minds through Christ Jesus. (Philippians 4:7)

The Lord Himself will fill us with astonishment and confusion of heart. (Deuteronomy 28:28) The Lord Himself will give us a heart of trembling, a spirit of fear, and a mind of sorrow. (Deuteronomy 28:65) Fear, worry, and depression will be an all-consuming curse upon us day and night. (Deuteronomy 28:66-67) The Lord Himself will cause us to *"cry for sorrow of heart"* and to *"howl for vexation of spirit."* (Isaiah 65:14) Thereby this way of forsaking the Lord in unrepentant wickedness and rebellion will be found only to be a bitter way that reaches into the depths of our heart with bitterness. *"There is no peace, saith my God, to the wicked."*

Let us then take heed unto our hearts that we not stubbornly continue in unrepentant rebellion. Rather, with a contrite and humble spirit, let us be quick to repent of our sinful iniquity and to return unto the Lord our God. This is the loving desire of our gracious Lord – not that the wicked should be destroyed in his wickedness, but that he should repent and be spiritually revived.

In Ezekiel 18:30-32 our Lord revealed His heart's desire concerning His own people, saying, *"Therefore I will judge you, O house of Israel, every one according to his ways, saith the Lord GOD. Repent, and turn yourselves from all your transgressions; so iniquity shall not be your ruin. Cast away from you all your transgressions, whereby ye have transgressed; and make you a new heart and a new spirit: for why will ye die, O house of Israel? For I have no pleasure in the death of him that dieth, saith the Lord GOD: wherefore turn yourselves, and live ye."*

Again in Ezekiel 33:10-11 He declared, *"Therefore, O thou son of man, speak unto the house of Israel; Thus ye speak, saying, If our transgressions and our sins be upon us, and we pine away in them, how should we then live? Say unto them, As I live, saith the Lord GOD, I have no pleasure in the death of the wicked; but that the wicked turn from his way and live: turn ye, turn ye from your evil ways; for why will ye die, O house of Israel?"* Even so, in love and grace our Lord calls forth unto us today – "Wherefore turn yourselves, and live ye!"

James 4:1-10

From whence come wars and fightings among you?
Come they not hence,
even of your lusts that war in your members?
Ye lust, and have not:
ye kill, and desire to have, and cannot obtain:
ye fight and war, yet ye have not, because ye ask not.
Ye ask, and receive not, because ye ask amiss,
that ye may consume it upon your lusts.
Ye adulterers and adulteresses, know ye not
that the friendship of the world is enmity with God?
Whosoever therefore will be a friend of the world
is the enemy of God.
Do ye think that the scripture saith in vain,
The spirit that dwelleth in us lusteth to envy?
But he giveth more grace.
Wherefore he saith, God resisteth the proud,
but giveth grace unto the humble.
Submit yourselves therefore to God.
Resist the devil, and he will flee from you.
Draw nigh to God, and he will draw nigh to you.
Cleanse your hands, ye sinners;
and purify your hearts, ye double minded.
Be afflicted, and mourn, and weep:
let your laughter be turned to mourning, and your joy to heaviness.
Humble yourselves in the sight of the Lord,
and he shall lift you up.

Chapter Six

Draw Nigh to God

With the opening line of James 4:8, we find a wonderful promise from the Lord our God – "***Draw nigh to God, and he will draw nigh to you.***" The Lord God of heaven and earth, the almighty Creator of all, "***the high and lofty One, that inhabiteth eternity, whose name is Holy,***" is willing to draw nigh unto each one of us individually in personal fellowship, if we will draw nigh unto Him according to His required standard. What greater blessing could possibly be granted to us!

Now, this principle and promise stands true for anyone, whether that one is taking the first steps in drawing nigh unto the Lord our God, or is maintaining a continual walk of drawing nigh unto the Lord our God. If we will draw nigh unto the Lord, He *will* draw nigh unto us; and the more that we draw nigh unto the Lord, the *more* He will draw nigh unto us.

Yet in the context of James 4:8, this principle and promise was not written to those who were already drawing nigh unto the Lord, in order to encourage them to remain faithful and to draw nearer. Rather, this principle and promise was written to believers who were walking at enmity with God through their selfishness and worldliness. In verses 1-4 a severe rebuke had been laid to their charge – "***From whence come wars and fightings among you? Come they not hence, even of your lusts that war in your members? Ye lust, and have not: ye kill, and desire to have, and cannot obtain: ye fight*** *and war, yet ye have not, because ye ask not. Ye ask, and receive not, because ye ask amiss, that ye may consume it upon your lusts. Ye adulterers and adulteresses, know ye not that the friendship of the world is enmity with God? Whosoever therefore will be a friend of the world is the enemy of God."*

To just such selfish, worldly believers, God's Word gives the instruction of verse 8 – *"Draw nigh to God;"* and to those among them who will do so, God's Word gives the promise – *"And he will draw nigh to you."* So then, what does it mean for a selfish, worldly believer to draw nigh unto the Lord our God?

Returning unto the Lord

In the context of James 4, this drawing nigh unto God is not the drawing closer of one who is already in fellowship with the Lord. Rather, this drawing nigh unto God is a *returning* unto the Lord by one who has been going away backward from Him. It is a turning away from our sinful ways and a returning unto our Lord's fellowship. It is a forsaking of our worldly ways and our fleshly desires. It is a seeking after our Lord to receive His abundant pardon, to submit unto His holy will, and to serve Him with all our heart.

It is the truth and instruction of Isaiah 55:6-7 – *"Seek ye the LORD while he may be found, call ye upon him while he is near: let the wicked forsake his way, and the unrighteous man his thoughts: and let him return unto the LORD, and he will have mercy upon him; and to our God, for he will abundantly pardon."*

It is the same as the Lord's call unto Israel in Jeremiah 3:12 – *"Go and proclaim these words toward the north, and say, Return, thou backsliding Israel, saith the LORD; and I will not cause mine anger to fall upon you: for I am merciful, saith the LORD, and I will not keep anger for ever."* Again it is the same as the Lord's call unto Israel in Joel 2:12-13 – *"Therefore also now, saith the LORD, turn ye even to me with all your heart, and with fasting, and with weeping, and with mourning: and rend your heart, and not your garments, and turn unto the LORD your God: for he is gracious and merciful, slow to anger, and of great kindness, and repenteth him of the evil."*

It is the same as the message delivered unto Israel in Hosea 6:1 – *"Come, and let us return unto the LORD: for he hath torn, and he will heal us; he hath smitten, and he will bind us up."* Again it is the same as the message delivered unto Israel in Hosea 14:1-2 – *"O Israel, return unto the LORD thy God; for thou hast fallen by thine iniquity. Take with you words, and turn to the LORD: say unto him, Take away all iniquity, and receive us graciously: so will we render the calves of our lips."* Yet again it is the same as the message delivered unto Israel in Zechariah 1:3 – *"Therefore say thou unto them, Thus saith the LORD of hosts; Turn ye unto me, saith the LORD of hosts, and I will turn unto you, saith the LORD of hosts."*

Repentance of Sin

Even so, this drawing nigh unto the Lord our God involves repentance of all sinful conduct and character. In James 4:8 the instruction of God's Word continues, *"Draw nigh to God, and he will draw nigh to you. Cleanse your hands, ye sinners; and purify your hearts, ye double minded."*

We must repent, and turn ourselves from all our transgressions. (Ezekiel 18:30) Yea, we must cast away all our transgressions, whereby we have transgressed against the Lord; and we must make us a new heart and a new spirit, a righteous heart and an obedient spirit. (Ezekiel 18:31) We must thoroughly amend our sinful ways and our sinful doings. (Jeremiah 7:5) We must wash ourselves and make ourselves clean spiritually. We must put away the evil of our ways and doings from before our Lord's eyes. (Isaiah 1:16) We must return from our evil way and must make our ways and our doings good and righteous in our Lord's sight. (Jeremiah 18:11)

We must honestly face and acknowledge the sin in our lives. Yet we must not simply acknowledge the sins of our outward actions and conduct, but also the sins of our inward attitudes and character. According to James 4:8 we must cleanse our hands (our outward actions and conduct) and must purify our hearts (our inward attitudes and character). We must forsake *both* our wicked ways *and* our unrighteous thoughts. (Isaiah 55:7) We must not be as the hypocrites, who *"make clean the outside of the cup and of the platter,"* but within are full of all uncleanness. (Matthew 23:25-28) Rather, we must *"cleanse ourselves from all filthiness of the flesh and spirit."* (2 Corinthians 7:1) Yes, we must cleanse ourselves from *all* the filthiness of *both* our flesh *and* our spirit.

However, we do not actually possess within ourselves the power to cleanse and purify ourselves. Only the Lord our God, through the shed blood of our Lord and Savior Jesus Christ, possesses the spiritual power to cleanse and purify us from our sin. (1 John 1:7) Yet we do indeed have a responsibility in the matter. The Lord our God has determined to cleanse and purify us *only* when we will confess our sins with a spirit of repentance. Our responsibility and our Lord's work in the matter are clearly revealed in 1 John 1:9 – *"If we confess our sins, he is faithful and just to forgive us our sins, and to cleanse us from all unrighteousness."*

Our responsibility in the matter is to come unto the ground of cleansing through the confession of our sins. Our Lord's work in the matter is to cleanse from all unrighteousness through the cleansing power of Christ's shed blood. We must come and reason together in full agreement with the Lord against our sin. (Isaiah 1:18) Then He will wash us thoroughly from our iniquity and cleanse us completely from our sin. (Psalm 51:2) Yea, upon the ground of our broken-hearted confession, through the cleansing power of Christ's shed blood, although spiritually our sins may be as a dark, scarlet stain upon us, we shall be made whiter than snow in our Lord's sight. (Isaiah 1:18)

Brokenness over Sin

Yet our confession of sin must indeed be that of a truly broken and contrite heart. *"The sacrifices of God are a broken spirit: a broken and a contrite heart, O God, thou wilt not despise."* (Psalm 51:17) Therefore, in James 4:8-9 the instruction of God's Word continues, *"Draw nigh to God, and he will draw nigh to you. Cleanse your hands, ye sinners; and purify your hearts, ye double minded. Be afflicted, and mourn, and weep: let your laughter be turned to mourning, and your joy to heaviness."*

Our hearts must be truly afflicted over the wickedness of our sin against the Lord our God. Our spirits must mourn and weep with spiritual brokenness over the iniquity of our unrighteousness in the sight of our Lord. The laughter and enjoyment that we had in the ungodly pleasures of sin must be turned to mourning and grief over the recognition that we have greatly offended the Lord our God and Savior.

We must be as the publican who *"would not lift up so much as his eyes unto heaven,"* but in utter brokenness and deep grief *"smote upon his breast, saying, God be merciful to me a sinner."* (Luke 18:13) We must be *"like doves of the valleys,"* mourning over the iniquity of our sin. (Ezekiel 7:16) We must be deeply grieved, horrified, and ashamed in heart that we have grieved the Lord our God by our transgressions and rebellion. As did the prophet Isaiah, so we must cry out in brokenness unto the Lord, *"Woe is me! For I am undone."* (Isaiah 6:5)

We must be sorry for our sin. (Psalm 38:18) Yet we must be sorry *"after a godly manner,"* in accord with God's purpose. (2 Corinthians 7:9) We must not simply be sorry (have sorrow) over the consequences of our sin. Rather, we must be sorry (have sorrow) over the offensiveness of our sin against the Lord and over the unrighteousness of our sin in the sight of the Lord. *"For godly sorrow worketh repentance to salvation not to be repented of: but the sorrow of the world worketh death."* (1 Corinthians 7:10)

We must be careful and eager to get right with the Lord. We must confess our sins and seek His merciful forgiveness and cleansing. We must have righteous indignation, bitterness, and hatred against our own sins. We must tremble with reverence and fear at the reproof and rebuke of God's Word and at the chastening and correction of God's hand. We must have a vehement desire to walk again in our Lord's fellowship with a clean heart and a right spirit. We must have zealous hunger and thirst to obey our Lord and pursue righteousness. We must take revenge against our sinful flesh by forsaking and mortifying our sinful ways.

Humility before the Lord

In all these things, we must repent of our sin and return unto our Lord with godly humility. In James 4:10 the instruction of God's Word concludes, **"Humble yourselves in the sight of the Lord, and he shall lift you up."** In this context, this is not the humility of a submissive walk, but of a repentant heart. Certainly a heart that is truly repentant should and will lead to a walk that is submissive. Yet, in this context, the instruction of this verse is specifically directed to us believers who need our hands cleansed and our hearts purified.

We must return unto the Lord with the recognition that we are completely unworthy and sinfully wicked in His sight. We must humbly accept the full responsibility, corruption, and punishment of our sin. We must bow before our Lord with a complete dependence upon His abundant grace, tender mercy, and loving kindness. We must wholly submit ourselves unto the Lord to serve Him with all our heart and soul. We must humble ourselves in the sight of the Lord over our sinfulness; and if we will, *then* He will lift us up with spiritual revival. This is our Lord's promise. Spiritual revival is Biblically *certain* to those of us who will so humble ourselves in repentance. On the other hand, it is also Biblically certain that we will *not* know spiritual revival *until* we so humble ourselves in broken-hearted repentance.

Chapter Seven

Enmity with God

As we considered in the previous chapter, in James 4:8-10 the believers to whom James was writing under the inspiration of the Holy Spirit were instructed to draw nigh unto God by humbling themselves before the Lord in broken-hearted repentance over their sinfulness. Their hands needed spiritual cleansing, and their hearts needed spiritual purifying. They had gone away backward from the Lord their God into sinful iniquity, and they were walking at enmity with God. They needed to repent of their sinful iniquity and to return unto the Lord their God. If they did return and draw near unto God, He promised that He would draw near unto them. If they did humble themselves before the Lord, He promised that He would lift them up to the high and holy place of His fellowship.

Yet what sin or sins in particular had put them at enmity with the Lord their God? The answer is found in James 4:1-5 – *"**From whence come wars and fightings among you? Come they not hence, even of your lusts that war in your members? Ye lust, and have not: ye kill, and desire to have, and cannot obtain: ye fight and war, yet ye have not, because ye ask not. Ye ask, and receive not, because ye ask amiss, that ye may consume it upon your lust. Ye adulterers and adulteresses, know ye not that the friendship of the world is enmity with God? Whosoever therefore will be a friend of the world is the enemy of God. Do ye think that the scripture saith in vain, The spirit that dwelleth in us lusteth to*** *envy?"* These believers were walking at spiritual enmity with God simply because they were walking in the sin of *selfishness and worldliness*.

Our Lusts that War in Our Members

The opening portion of James 4:1 presents the question, ***"From whence come wars and fightings among you?"*** What is the true, foundational source for the conflicts, contentions, strifes, divisions, fights, arguments, etc. that flare up so often and so easily among us? The closing portion of James 4:1 reveals the answer, ***"Come they not hence, even of your lusts that war in your members?"*** The foundational source for all our spirit of contention and strife is the element of selfish lust within our hearts that ever seeks to control us and drive us in its way. It is that indwelling element of selfish, fleshly lust that wars against our purified souls. (1 Peter 2:11)

Now, in this context the word "lusts" does not refer simply to a driving desire for sexual gratification. Rather, in this context the word "lusts" refers more broadly to a driving desire for anything that would please one's self. It refers to our *selfish* motivations. Even so, the opening portion of verse 2 provides an explanation, saying, ***"Ye lust, and have not: ye kill, and desire to have, and cannot obtain."*** This lust is the "desire to have." It is the driving desire to have whatever we selfishly want.

This is the motivation that moves us to fight and war in order to get and obtain our own way. This is the motivation that moves us to go astray from our Lord. (Isaiah 53:6) This is the motivation that moves us to strive with self-importance and self-dependence to acquire our own desires and to accomplish our own purposes, rather than to pray with Biblical humility in dependence upon our Lord. ***"Ye fight and war, yet ye have not, because ye ask not."***

Such selfish motivation is the reason that we are walking at enmity with the Lord our God. In selfishness, we will not deny ourselves, and take up our cross daily, and follow our Lord. (Luke 9:23) In selfishness, we will not lose our lives for our Lord's sake; but we strive to save our lives for our own sake. (Luke 9:24) In selfishness, we will not present ourselves as *"a living sacrifice, holy, acceptable unto God."* (Romans 12:1) In selfishness, we will not live wholly unto our Lord who died for us; but we live unto ourselves, walking after the selfish desires of our sinful flesh. (2 Corinthians 5:15) This is enmity with God.

In selfishness, we even pray unto the Lord, seeking for Him to serve our will and pleasure; yet He will not hear us. *"Ye ask, and receive not, because ye ask amiss, that ye may consume it upon your lust."* Even our prayers for spiritual revival and the filling of the Holy Spirit are often rooted in selfishness, not truly for the purpose of our Lord's will and glory, but to be consumed upon our selfish desire for self-advancement, self-accomplishment, and self-acclaim. This is enmity with God.

Friendship with the World and Its Ways

In addition, such selfish motivation moves us to set our love and affection upon the things of this present evil world. In James 4:4 the severe rebuke of God's Holy Word is delivered against such selfish believers, saying, *"Ye adulterers and adulteresses, know ye not that the friendship of the world is enmity with God? Whosoever therefore will be a friend of the world is the enemy of God."* Herein the two words "friendship" and "friend" indicate a relationship of affection and love for this world, of fellowship and unity with this world.

Concerning such affection for this world, Colossians 3:1-3 gives us the instruction, *"If ye then be risen with Christ, seek those things which are above, where Christ sitteth on the right hand of God. Set your affection on things above, not on things on the earth. For ye are dead* [that is – spiritually dead to sin through newness of life in Christ], *and your life is hid with Christ in God."* Spiritually there are only two possible ways in which we might direct the affection of our hearts and the focus of our minds. Either we will direct our affection and focus "on things above," which is a characteristic of fellowship with the Lord our God; or we will direct our affection and focus "on things on the earth," which is a characteristic of friendship with this present evil world.

In like manner, 1 John 2:15-17 gives us the instruction, *"Love not the world, neither the things that are in the world. If any man love the world, the love of the Father is not in him. For all that is in the world, the lust of the flesh, and the lust of the eyes, and the pride of life, is not of the Father, but is of the world. And the world passeth away, and the lust thereof: but he that doeth the will of God abideth for ever."* Spiritually there are only two ways in which we might direct the love of our hearts. Either we will direct our love toward this world and "the things that are in this world," or we will direct our love toward God our heavenly Father. At any given time, if we direct the love of our hearts toward this world and the things of this world, then at that given time, love for God our heavenly Father is not abiding in our hearts.

Furthermore, in 1 John 2:16 God's Word classifies *"all that is in the world"* as *"the lust of the flesh, and the lust of the eyes, and the pride of life."* These classifications reveal that the problem is not in the *objects* of this world in and of themselves, but in our *motivations* toward the objects of this world. The first two of these classifications employ the word "lust," which here refers to a driving, selfish desire. The third of these classifications employs the word "pride," which here refers to an arrogant self-confidence. These are terms of heart-motivation.

Thus "the lust of the flesh" refers to a driving, selfish desire for the *pleasures* of this life. "The lust of the eyes" refers to a driving, selfish desire for the *possessions* of this life." "The pride of life" refers to a driving, selfish pursuit after personal *promotion* in this life, whether it be the promotion of our *priorities* and *purposes* over God's will, or the promotion of *popularity* and *prestige* among others, or the promotion of *praise* from others, or the promotion of *position* above others, or the promotion of *power* over others, etc. These heart-motivations are not of the Lord our God and heavenly Father, but of this present, evil world. These are the heart-motivations of worldliness. These are the heart-motivations that characterize the friendship of this world. These are the heart-motivations that cause the enmity of the Lord our God to be against us.

Enmity with God Our Heavenly Father

In James 4:4 we find two sets of contrasting words, and they are employed in a clear principle of separation. First, we find the two words "friendship" and "enmity." Second, we find the two words "friend" and "enemy." *"Friendship of the world is enmity with God;"* and to be *"a friend of the world"* is to be *"the enemy of God."* This is a universal, eternal principle without any exception.

In like manner, we must understand the opposite principle – Friendship with God requires enmity of the world; and to be the friend of God (that is – to walk in daily fellowship with the Lord our God), we must be the enemy of this present, evil world. There is no middle ground in this spiritual matter. We *cannot* set our love and affection upon the lust of the flesh, the lust of the eyes, and the pride of life, and set our love and affection upon God our heavenly Father at the same time. It is spiritually *impossible*. We *cannot* serve and follow after both. At any given moment in our daily Christian walk, we must choose one or the other.

Even so, our Lord Jesus Christ declared in Matthew 6:24, *"No man can serve two masters: for either he will hate the one, and love the other; or else he will hold to the one, and despise the other. Ye cannot serve God and mammon* [the things of this world]." According to this principle, if we love this present, evil world, then by definition we *hate* God our heavenly Father; and according to this principle, if we hold to this present, evil world, then by definition we *despise* God our heavenly Father. *"Whosoever therefore will be a friend of the world is the enemy of God."*

Cheating on Jesus Christ Our Savior

In James 4:4 the rebuke of God's Holy Word against those believers who have entered into the friendship of this world begins with the phrase, *"Ye adulterers and adulteresses."* In this context, this phrase is not a reference to the sin of physical adultery, but to the sin of *spiritual* adultery. In this context, this is not a reference to our cheating on our marriage relationships with our spouses. Rather, this is a reference to our cheating on our fellowship relationship *with our Lord*.

The friendship of this world is spiritual adultery against our spiritual Husband. Who then is our spiritual Husband? The apostle revealed the answer in 2 Corinthians 11:2, saying, "***For I am jealous over you with godly jealousy: for I have espoused you to one husband, that I may present you as a chaste virgin to Christ.***" In like manner, the truth is revealed in Ephesians 5:25-27, "***Husbands, love your wives, even as Christ also loved the church, and gave himself for it; that he might sanctify and cleanse it with the washing of water by the word, that he might present it to himself a glorious church, not having spot, or wrinkle, or any such thing; but that it should be holy and without blemish.***"

The church, consisting of true believers, is the espoused bride of Christ. Yea, we who are believers in God the Son, the Lord Jesus Christ, as our eternal Savior are the espoused bride of Christ. Our Lord and Savior Jesus Christ, our espoused Husband, "***gave himself for our sins, that he might deliver us from this present evil world, according to the will of God and our Father.***" (Galatians 1:4) He "***gave himself for us, that he might redeem us from all iniquity.***" (Titus 2:14) He gave himself for us that He might present us unto Himself as a glorious bride, being completely holy and without spiritual blemish. Thus when we turn our love and affection away from Him, who is our spiritual Husband, and give our love and affection to the world, from which He delivered us, we commit spiritual adultery against Him

An Offense to the Indwelling Holy Spirit

In James 4:5 the rebuke of God's Holy Word continues yet the more, saying, "***Do ye think that the scripture saith in vain, The spirit that dwelleth in us lusteth to envy?***" At the very moment of our faith in Christ for salvation, God the Holy Spirit came to indwell our spirit.

Even so, Galatians 3:13-14 states, "***Christ hath redeemed us from the curse of the law, being made a curse for us: for it is written, Cursed is every one that hangeth on a tree: that the blessing of Abraham might come on the Gentiles through Jesus Christ; that*** *we might receive the promise of the Spirit through faith.*" In addition, Galatians 4:4-6 states, *"But when the fulness of the time was come, God sent forth his Son, made of a woman, made under the law, to redeem them that were under the law, that we might receive the adoption of sons. And because ye are sons, God hath sent forth the Spirit of his Son into your hearts, crying, Abba, Father."*

Now throughout our daily walk, the indwelling Holy Spirit of God ever seeks to direct us in God's way of holiness and righteousness. Yet when we choose to follow after selfishness and worldliness, we quench His righteous guidance in our lives and grieve His holy heart. Yea, by choosing to follow after the selfish, worldly desires of our sinful flesh, we greatly offend the indwelling *Holy* Spirit of God. He is holy and righteous by nature, and our selfishness and worldliness offends His holy, righteous nature.

Our bodies and spirits are the temple of the indwelling Holy Spirit. We are not our own. We are bought with the price of Christ's precious blood. (1 Corinthians 6:19-20) Thus the indwelling Holy Spirit has every right to expect a spiritually clean and holy temple in which to dwell. He has every right to expect us to be clean from all spiritual filthiness and to be *"perfecting holiness in the fear of God."* (2 Corinthians 7:1) He has every right to expect us to separate ourselves from the unclean motivations of selfishness and worldliness and to glorify the Lord our God in our body and in our spirit, *"which are God's."* (1 Corinthians 6:20)

Yet the indwelling Holy Spirit not only expects such behavior from us, but also longs greatly and earnestly after such a relationship with us. His heart is wholly invested in our fellowship with and our submission to God our heavenly Father and Jesus Christ our Lord. Therefore, when we give ourselves to walk after selfishness and worldliness instead, the indwelling Holy Spirit is moved to righteous jealousy and envy over our departure from a right relationship with Him. He is moved to righteous jealousy and envy whenever our love and affection is turned away from God our heavenly Father and Jesus Christ our Lord unto our selfish, sinful flesh and this present, evil world.

This is the reason that, when we are walking in selfish ways and worldly motivations, we are instructed to draw nigh unto the Lord our God. These selfish ways and worldly motivations cause us to go away backward from the Lord our God. They cause us to walk at enmity with Him, and they cause Him to stand at enmity against us. They cause Him to resist us with His hand of chastening. Thus we are called to turn back from our selfishness and worldliness unto the Lord our God. *"**Draw nigh to God, and he will draw nigh to you. Cleanse your hands, ye sinners; and purify your hearts, ye double minded. Be afflicted, and mourn, and weep: let our laughter be turned to mourning, and your joy to heaviness. Humble yourselves in the sight of the Lord, and he shall lift you up.**"* (James 4:8-10)

Chapter Eight

But He Giveth More Grace

Although we may have gone away backward spiritually from the Lord our God through the sinful iniquity of our own selfishness and worldliness, He continually offers to revive us, restore us, and renew us again by His grace. Moment by moment the truth of God's Word from James 4:6 is brought to the attention of our hearts by the Holy Spirit, "***But he giveth more grace.***"

Out of the motivation of selfishness, we may have been continually fighting among ourselves to get our own way; but *He* giveth more grace. Through the selfishness of our hearts, we may have been striving with self-importance and self-dependence to get, while neglecting to pray in humble dependence upon God; but He *giveth* more grace. By our selfishness and worldliness, our very prayers may have been corrupted and defiled in our Lord's sight; but He giveth *more* grace. Because of our worldly character and conduct, we may have been walking at enmity with the Lord our God; but He giveth more *grace*. Where our sin does abound, His grace does much more abound.

Yet the abundance of our Lord God's grace is only granted unto those who will humble themselves before Him and walk in humility with Him. The closing portion of James 4:6 declares, "***Wherefore he saith, God resisteth the proud, but giveth grace unto the humble.***" The Lord our God will not revive us spiritually through His more abundant grace as long as we continue in the pride of our self-centered, self-dependent, self-serving, and self-exalting ways. He will not bestow His more abundant grace upon the proud. As long as we walk in the pride of selfishness, our Lord will continually resist us and stand at enmity against us.

On the other hand, the Lord our God will indeed pour out His more abundant grace upon the humble. In the context of James 4:6-10, this is revealed more fully through the three conditional promises of verse 7, verse 8, and verse 10.

In verses 1-5 a rebuke was delivered against the spiritual condition of the believers to whom James was writing under the inspiration of God the Holy Spirit. This spiritual condition was one of enmity with God because of their selfishness and worldliness. Then in verses 6-7 a description is revealed concerning what their spiritual condition should have been. It should have been one of spiritual victory through humble submission to God. Finally, in verses 8-10 the way is presented by which they might correct their spiritual condition from what it was to what it ought to be. Thus, in the practice of our daily walk, the correctives and conditional promises of verses 8-10 must precede the character and conditional promise of verse 7.

Grace for Spiritual Restoration

In James 4:8 the conditional promise is given, "*Draw nigh to God, and he will draw nigh to you.*" This is the promise of God's grace for spiritual restoration to those who will humble themselves in repentance before Him.

As we have noted in a previous chapter, this instruction to draw nigh unto God was not delivered to believers who were already walking in fellowship with the Lord their God, in order to encourage them to draw even closer in fellowship unto Him. Rather, this instruction was delivered to believers who were walking at enmity against the Lord their God, in order to exhort them to turn from their sinful ways and to return unto the Lord. In this context, the instruction to draw nigh unto the Lord our God is a call to broken-hearted repentance of our selfishness and worldliness. Even so, verses 8-9 continue the instruction, saying, "*Draw nigh to God, and he will draw nigh to you.*

Cleanse your hands, ye sinners; and purify your hearts, ye double minded. Be afflicted, and mourn, and weep: let your laughter be turned to mourning, and your joy to heaviness."

What then is the promise that the Lord our God proclaims unto all of us who will indeed repent of our sinful ways before Him? The condition is that we must draw nigh unto the Lord our God through broken-hearted repentance. The condition is that we must cleanse our hands and purify our hearts of our sinful iniquity and stubborn rebellion. The condition is that we must willingly turn away from our sinful ways, doings, and thoughts. The condition is that we must humbly turn again unto the Lord our God. Then the promise is that He will give grace unto the humble. The promise is that He will draw nigh unto us in abundant grace with spiritual restoration.

In the first place, the Lord our God will graciously grant us abundant pardon. In Isaiah 55:6-7 the instruction and promise is given, *"Seek ye the LORD while he may be found, call ye upon him while he is near: let the wicked forsake his way, and the un-righteous man his thoughts: and let him return unto the LORD, and he will have mercy upon him; and to our God, for he will abundantly pardon."* If we will draw nigh unto Him in repentance of our sin, the Lord our God will abundantly pardon us in the abundance of His grace. He will pardon the sinful iniquity of our selfishness and worldliness according unto the greatness of His mercy.

He is good, and ready to forgive us our sins the very moment that we humble ourselves to turn and draw nigh unto Him in repentance. (Psalm 86:5) *"For as the heaven is high above the earth, so great is his mercy toward them that fear him* [that is – toward them who will humble themselves in repentance before Him]." (Psalm 103:11) Yea, *"as far as the east is from the west,"* so far will He, in the abundant pardon of His abundant grace and mercy, remove our transgressions and our sins from us. (Psalm 103:12) Therefore, the prophet Micah exclaimed in Micah 7:18-19, *"Who is a God like unto thee, that pardoneth iniquity, and passeth by the transgression of the remnant of his heritage? He retaineth not his anger for ever, because he delighteth in mercy. He will turn again, he will have compassion upon us; he will subdue our iniquities; and thou wilt cast all their sins into the depths of the sea."*

In the second place, the Lord our God will graciously restore us to His blessed fellowship. He will not simply bestow His pardon upon us; He Himself will draw nigh in fellowship unto us. He will dwell in the high and holy place of His blessed fellowship with those of us who will come to a contrite and humble spirit of repentance before Him. (Isaiah 57:15) Yea, He Himself will lift us up out of the horrible pit and miry clay of our sin unto the high and holy place of His fellowship. (Psalm 40:2)

If we will humbly turn unto Him, He will graciously turn unto us. He will take away all our iniquity and will receive us graciously. (Hosea 14:2) He will heal our spiritual backsliding and will love us freely in a walk of intimate fellowship. (Hosea 14:4) He will speak unto us *"**with good words and comfortable words.**"* (Zechariah 1:13) He will be unto us *"**a wall of fire round about**"* and will be *"**the glory in the midst**"* of our hearts and lives. (Zechariah 2:5)

Grace for Spiritual Progress

Yet the Lord our God gives even *more* grace. In James 4:10 the conditional promise is given, *"**Humble yourselves in the sight of the Lord, and he shall lift you up.**"* This is the promise of God's grace for spiritual progress to those who will humble themselves in dependence upon Him.

We who have ensnared ourselves in the dark pit and miry clay of ungodliness, how shall we ever find deliverance out of that spiritual captivity? We who have invested our hearts and lives in the ways of unrighteousness, how shall we ever grow upward again in spiritual maturity? We who have gone away backward from our Lord into the corruption of sin, how shall we ever go forward again in the way of righteousness? We who have become spiritually withered in carnality and worldliness, how shall we ever bear spiritual fruit again unto the glory of our Lord? We who have corrupted ourselves in the filth of wickedness, how shall we ever be spiritually useful again in the work and ministry of our Lord?

Our hope and help is only and wholly to be found in the Lord our God and His more abundant grace. The prophet Jeremiah understood this truth; therefore, in Lamentations 3:21-24 he proclaimed,

"*This I recall to my mind, therefore have I hope. It is of the LORD'S mercies that we are not consumed, because his compassions fail not. They are new every morning: great is thy faithfulness. The LORD is my portion, saith my soul; therefore will I hope in him.*" In a time of grievous chastening from the Lord, the prophet humbled himself in the sight of the Lord and set his dependence wholly upon the overflowing mercies, unfailing compassion, and everlasting faithfulness of the Lord.

Even so, Jeremiah expressed his assurance in verses 25-26, saying, "*The LORD is good unto them that wait for him, to the soul that seeketh him. It is good that a man should both hope and quietly wait for the salvation of the LORD.*" In humble dependence he sought after the Lord. In humble dependence he set his hope in the Lord. In humble dependence he quietly (patiently) waited for the help and deliverance of the Lord. Therefore, in such humble dependence upon the Lord, he experienced the abundant grace and goodness of the Lord. This is the principle of God's Word – The Lord *is* good unto such individuals. It is not that the Lord shall be good unto them some time in the future. Rather, it is that the Lord's goodness is poured out upon them from the very moment of their humble dependence upon Him.

The man of God Daniel also understood this truth. In Daniel 9:5-6 Daniel confessed the sinful iniquity and stubborn rebellion of himself and his people, saying, "*We have sinned, and have committed iniquity, and have done wickedly, and have rebelled, even by departing from thy precepts and from thy judgments: neither have we hearkened unto thy servants the prophets, which spake in thy name to our kings, our princes, and our fathers, and to all the people of the land.*" Yet he expressed his assurance in verse 9 – "*To the Lord our God belong mercies and forgivenesses, though we have rebelled against him.*"

Therefore, in verses 18-19 Daniel set his humble dependence upon the Lord through prayer, saying, "*O my God, incline thine ear, and hear; open thine eyes, and behold our desolations, and the city which is called by thy name: for we do not present our supplications before thee for our righteousnesses, but for thy great mercies. O Lord, hear; O Lord, forgive; O Lord, hearken and do; defer not, for thine own sake, O my God: for thy city and thy people are called by thy name."*

In like manner, while under the heavy hand of the Lord's chastening, the man of God David cried out in Psalm 38:1-4, *"O LORD, rebuke me not in thy wrath: neither chasten me in thy hot displeasure. For thine arrows stick fast in me, and thy hand presseth me sore. There is no soundness in my flesh because of thine anger; neither is there any rest in my bones because of my sin. For mine iniquities are gone over mine head: as an heavy burden they are too heavy for me."*

At such a time, where did David set his hope and dependence? In verse 15 he gives answer, *"For in thee, O LORD, do I hope: thou wilt hear, O Lord my God."* First, he expressed broken-hearted repentance of his sin through confession in verse 18 – *"For I will declare mine iniquity; I will be sorry for my sin."* Then he expressed humble dependence upon the Lord through prayer in verses 21-22 – *"Forsake me not, O LORD: O my God, be not far from me. Make haste to help me, O Lord my salvation."* He set His hope in the Lord as his one way of deliverance from the corruption and consequences of his sin. With humble dependence on the Lord, he had full assurance of faith that the Lord would hear the cry of his prayer and would make haste to help him.

What then is the promise that the Lord our God proclaims unto all of us who will indeed humble ourselves in dependence upon Him? The condition is that we must humble ourselves in the sight of the Lord through whole-hearted dependence. The condition is that we must set our hope completely in the abundant grace, overflowing mercies, unfailing compassions, almighty goodness, and everlasting faithfulness of the Lord our God. The condition is that we must fervently pray and quietly wait with full assurance of faith in our gracious Lord. Then the promise is that He will give grace unto the humble. The promise is that He will lift us up by His abundant grace for renewed spiritual progress.

In Psalm 40:1-4 the man of God David gave testimony, saying, "*I waited patiently for the LORD; and he inclined unto me, and heard my cry. He brought me up also out of an horrible pit, out of the miry clay, and set my feet upon a rock, and established my goings. And he hath put a new song in my mouth, even praise unto our God: many shall see it, and fear, and shall trust in the LORD. Blessed is that man that maketh the LORD his trust, and respecteth not the proud, nor such as turn aside to lies.*"

When we are in the horrible pit and miry clay of our own wickedness, when our sinful iniquities have taken hold upon us, so that we are unable to see any escape and so that our heart fails within us (Psalm 40:12), then we must humbly make the Lord our trust. If we will, then He will graciously hear our cry and will graciously deliver us out of the horrible pit and miry clay of our iniquity.

Yet in the abundance of His grace, our Lord will do more. First, He will set our feet upon a rock as the strong, stable foundation for our renewed spiritual growth. Yea, He will plant us firmly in the grace of His fellowship, the truth of His Word, and the guidance of His Spirit. Second, He will establish our goings through His leading in a renewed walk after righteousness. Yea, He Himself will graciously lead us "*in the paths of righteousness for his name's sake.*" (Psalm 23:3)

Third, He will do a transforming work within us for our renewed fruitfulness in every good work. Yea, He will graciously renew within us a right spirit of mind and will graciously put a new song in our hearts, even praise unto the Lord our God. Finally, He will sanctify us and make us meet for a renewed usefulness in His work and ministry. Yea, by His grace many shall be moved through the testimony and witness of our lives to fear Him and to trust in Him.

Grace for Spiritual Victory

Yet the Lord our God gives even *more abundant* grace. In James 4:7 the conditional promise is given, "*Submit yourselves therefore to God. Resist the devil, and he will flee from you.*" This is the promise of God's grace for spiritual victory to those who will humble themselves in submission to Him.

This promise for spiritual victory over our adversary the devil actually includes a two-fold condition. The condition that is directly connected to the promise is that we must resist the devil. In like manner, 1 Peter 5:8-9 gives the instruction, *"**Be sober, be vigilant; because your adversary the devil, as a roaring lion, walketh about, seeking whom he may devour: whom resist stedfast in the faith, knowing that the same afflictions are accomplished in your brethren that are in the world.**"* Certainly we must be sober and vigilant at all times to stand against the wiles and temptations of the devil. Certainly we must steadfastly resist the fiery darts and fierce attacks of the devil against our daily Christian walk.

Yet we must not attempt to resist the devil in our own strength and ability. Rather, we must *"**be strong in the grace that is in Christ Jesus.**"* (2 Timothy 2:1) We must *"**be strong in the Lord, and in the power of his might,**"* and must *"**put on the whole armour of God,**"* in order that we may be able to stand with steadfast resistance *"**against the wiles of the devil.**"* (Ephesians 6:10-11) Only through the almighty power of the Lord our God will we be able to stand victorious against our adversary the devil. Only the almighty power of the Lord our God is able to make the devil flee from us.

Therefore, it is necessary that we consider the first instruction of James 4:7 as a foundational condition to the second instruction and the resulting promise. We must first submit ourselves to the Lord our God before we will be able to resist the devil aright with divine power and certain victory. Yes, our adversary the devil will flee from us; and we will stand victorious in the evil day. Yet this will only occur when we resist the devil through humble submission to the lordship authority of the Lord our God over our hearts and lives.

We must humbly yield ourselves unto God and our members *"**as instruments of righteousness unto God.**"* (Romans 6:13) We must humbly present ourselves each day as *"**a living sacrifice, holy, acceptable unto God,**"* to serve Him and do His will whole-heartedly in our daily walk. (Romans 12:1) We must humbly take our Lord's yoke of service upon us, and learn of Him. (Matthew 11:29) We must deny ourselves, and take up our cross of submission daily, and humbly follow our Lord's direction in all things. (Luke 9:22)

This is the foundational condition for spiritual victory in our daily Christian walk – humble submission to the Lord. On the ground of this foundational submission, our Lord will empower us in and by His grace. Then we will be divinely empowered to resist our adversary the devil steadfastly in the faith, and then our adversary the devil will flee from us. When we humbly submit ourselves unto the Lord, He will fight for us; and when our Lord fights for us, we will know spiritual victory.

Chapter Nine

God Resisteth the Proud

As we consider the subject of spiritual revival, it must be understood that there can be *no* spiritual revival where the spirit of pride exists. The Lord our God promises *"to revive the spirit of the humble, and to revive the heart of the contrite ones."* (Isaiah 57:15) However, He does not revive, restore, or renew the proud. Rather, He promises to *resist* the proud. *"But God giveth more grace. Wherefore he saith, God resisteth the proud, but giveth grace to the humble."* (James 4:6)

The Spiritual Character of the Proud

The spirit of pride is a sinful spirit. Proverbs 21:4 declares, *"An high look, and a proud heart, and the plowing of the wicked, is sin."* The spirit of pride does not find its source in God our heavenly Father, but in this present evil world. In 1 John 2:16 God's Word reveals that *"the pride of life"* is included with *"the lust of the flesh"* and *"the lust of the eyes"* as the sinful characteristics of worldliness. It is out from this very worldliness, out from this very spirit of selfishness and pride, that we need to be revived spiritually.

True spiritual revival and a proud spirit cannot mix. Whenever we love and walk in the foundational motivations of worldliness, *"the lust of the flesh, and the lust of the eyes, and the pride of life,"* the love of God our heavenly Father is not the governing principle of our heart. (1 John 2:15) By its very nature, the spirit of pride will keep us from drawing nigh unto the Lord our God in humble repentance of our sin. By its very nature, the spirit of pride will turn us away from walking with the Lord our God through humble dependence and submission.

➢ The Pride of Self-Centeredness

By its very nature, the spirit of pride will motivate us unto a self-centered walk, rather than a God-centered walk. It will cause us to turn the focus of our thoughts and affection from the Lord our God to the comforts of this life. It will keep us from blessing the Lord our God for His goodness in our lives. It will cause us to take for granted every good gift that the Lord our God has given us by His abundant grace. It will keep us from acknowledging the Lord our God in all our ways and from obeying His will in our daily walk. It will cause us to take personal credit for the prosperities and progress of our lives. It will keep us from giving unto the Lord our God the glory due to His name.

Even so, in Deuteronomy 8:10-17 Moses warned the children of Israel, saying, *"When thou hast eaten and art full, then thou shalt bless the LORD thy God for the good land which he hath given thee. Beware that thou forget not the LORD thy God, in not keeping his commandments, and his judgments, and his statutes, which I command thee this day: lest when thou hast eaten and art full, and hast built goodly houses, and dwelt therein; and when thy herds and thy flocks multiply, and thy silver and thy gold is multiplied, and all that thou hast is multiplied; then thine heart be lifted up, and thou forget the LORD thy God, which brought thee forth out of the land of Egypt, from the house of bondage; who led thee through that great and terrible wilderness, wherein were fiery serpents, and scorpions, and drought, where there was no water; who brought thee forth water out of the rock of flint; who fed thee in the wilderness with manna, which thy fathers knew not, that he might humble thee, and that he might prove thee, to do thee good at thy latter end; and thou say in thine heart, My power and the might of mine hand hath gotten me this wealth."*

➢ **The Pride of Sinful Iniquity**

By its very nature, the spirit of pride will motivate us to walk in sinful iniquity, rather than in faithful godliness. It will cause us to walk after the sinful ways of the anointed cherub Lucifer, whose heart was lifted up with pride and who corrupted himself thereby. (Isaiah 14:12-16; Ezekiel 28:11-17) It will keep us from receiving, pursuing, and obeying the wholesome words of our Lord's Word and *"the doctrine which is according to godliness."* (1 Timothy 6:3-5) Rather, it will cause us to pursue anger, wrath, strife, and contention in our dealings with others. (Proverbs 13:10; 21:24; 28:25) Finally, it will keep us from ministering in godly love unto the edification of our fellow believers. (1 Corinthians 8:1)

➢ **The Pride of Stubborn Rebellion**

By its very nature, the spirit of pride will motivate us to walk in stubborn rebellion, rather than in humble repentance. It will cause us to boast confidently concerning the sinful desires of our heart. It will keep us from seeking after the Lord our God and from acknowledging His lordship in our lives. It will cause us always to walk in those ways that are grievous in the sight of the Lord our God. It will keep us from any consideration of the Lord's rebuke or judgment. It will convince us that we cannot be moved by any adversity.

Even so, Psalm 10:3-6 reveals the proud character of those who walk in stubborn rebellion, saying, *"For the wicked boasteth of his heart's desire, and blesseth the covetous, whom the LORD abhorreth. The wicked, through the pride of his countenance, will not seek after God: God is not in all his thoughts. His ways are always grievous; thy judgments are far above out of his sight: as for all his enemies, he puffeth at them. He hath said in his heart, I shall not be moved: for I shall never be in adversity."*

In addition, the spirit of pride will cause us to persecute those who are weaker or poorer than ourselves, to curse, deceive, and cheat others for selfish gain, and to speak highly, and thus wickedly, concerning oppression against others. Yea, the spirit of pride will convince us that we will never be caught, even by God Himself.

The opening portion of Psalm 10:2 declares, "*The wicked in his pride doth persecute the poor.*" To this verses 7-11 add, "*His mouth is full of cursing and deceit and fraud: under his tongue is mischief and vanity. He sitteth in the lurking places of the villages: in the secret places doth he murder the innocent: his eyes are privily set against the poor. He lieth in wait secretly as a lion in his den: he lieth in wait to catch the poor: he doth catch the poor, when he draweth him into his net. He croucheth, and humbleth himself, that the poor may fall by his strong ones. He hath said in his heart, God hath forgotten: he hideth his face; he will never see it.*" Finally, Psalm 73:8-9 states, "*They are corrupt, and speak wickedly concerning oppression: they speak loftily. They set their mouth against the heavens, and their tongue walketh through the earth.*"

> ### The Pride of Self-Righteousness

By its very nature, the spirit of pride will motivate us unto a self-righteous walk, rather than a God-submitted walk. It will cause us to be wise in our own conceit and to view our way as right in our own eyes. (Proverbs 12:15; 26:12) It will keep us from hearkening unto counsel and reproof, from fearing and submitting unto the Lord, and from departing away from evil. (Proverbs 3:7; 12:15; 14:16) It will cause us to be a wicked generation, "*that are pure in there own eyes, and yet is not washed from their filthiness.*" (Proverbs 30:12-13) It will keep us from the path of spiritual wisdom and health. (Proverbs 3:7-8; 14:16) It will lead us down the path of spiritual destruction. (Proverbs 16:25) Yea, it will cause us to face the woe of God's judgment as religious hypocrites, per-forming religious works, not out of love for the Lord our God, but out of love for the recognition, praise, and honor of men. (Matthew 23:5-7; Mark 12:38-40)

"*There is a generation, O how lofty are their eyes! And there eyelids are lifted up.*" (Proverbs 30:13) This is the generation of God's people who *need* spiritual revival.

The Lord's Resistance to the Proud

Again the truth is proclaimed – True spiritual revival and a proud spirit cannot mix. Again the principle of God's Word is quoted – *"God resisteth the proud, but giveth grace unto the humble."* (James 4:6) The Lord our God does not honor the spirit of pride with spiritual revival. Rather, He hates the spirit of pride as an abomination in His sight. (Proverbs 6:16-17) *"Every one that is proud in heart is an abomination to the LORD: though hand join in hand, he shall not be unpunished."* (Proverbs 16:5)

Concerning the great day of our Lord's judgment, Isaiah 2:11-12 declares, *"The lofty looks of man shall be humbled, and the haughtiness of men shall be bowed down, and the LORD alone shall be exalted in that day. For the day of the LORD of hosts shall be upon every one that is proud and lofty, and upon every one that is lifted up; and he shall be brought low."* Again in Isaiah 13:11 our Lord proclaimed, *"And I will punish the world for their evil, and the wicked for their iniquity; and I will cause the arrogancy of the proud to cease, and will lay low the haughtiness of the terrible."*

The Lord our God is not for the proud in heart, but against them. *"The LORD will destroy the house of the proud."* (Proverbs 15:25) The Lord will *"bring down high looks."* (Psalm 18:27) *"The LORD shall cut off all flattering lips, and the tongue that speaketh proud things."* (Psalm 12:3) The Lord *"plentifully rewardeth the proud doer"* with His judgment. (Psalm 31:23) The Lord will show *"strength with his arm"* and will scatter *"the proud in the imagination of their hearts."* (Luke 1:51)

The universal principle of God concerning the spirit of pride is clearly revealed in Matthew 23:12 – *"And whosoever shall exalt himself shall be abased; and he that shall humble himself shall be exalted."* The Lord our God will not revive us again when are walking in the spirit of pride, but will resist us continually. If we exalt ourselves with a spirit of pride, we shall be abased under our Lord's chastening hand. Only when we humble ourselves in the sight of the Lord, shall we be lifted up by His reviving hand.

The spirit of pride is *the great hindrance* to spiritual revival. When we are in need of spiritual revival, the spirit of pride will *prevent us from entering* into that path. So often the spirit of pride keeps us from the place of repentance before the Lord, of dependence upon the Lord, and of submission to the Lord. So often, in the spirit of pride, we are too self-centered, self-righteous, or stubbornly rebellions to humble ourselves in broken-hearted repentance, utter dependence, and complete submission.

In addition, the spirit of pride is *the great destroyer* of spiritual revival. When we have entered into the path of spiritual revival, the spirit of pride will *remove us from continuing* in that path. So often, after spiritual revival has begun in our lives, we are lifted up with the spirit of pride in or over some aspect of that revival; and thereby we lose our way on the path of revival. So often, in the spirit of pride, we may continue in the activities of revival and not even recognize that we have departed from the reality of revival.

The Biblical Warning against Pride

Even so, God's Word strongly warns us against the spirit of pride. In Proverbs 11:2 the warning is given, **"When pride cometh, then cometh shame: but with the lowly is wisdom."** The wisdom of true spiritual revival and true spiritual maturity shall only grow in the lives of the lowly. Yet when pride enters into our hearts, then we will be brought to spiritual shame before our Lord. Again in Proverbs 29:23 the warning is given, **"A man's pride shall bring him low: but honour shall uphold the humble in spirit."** The Lord our God shall graciously uphold those of a humble spirit in the high, holy, and honorable place of His reviving fellowship and favor. Yet a proud spirit will remove us from that high, holy, and honorable place and will bring us spiritually low.

In Proverbs 16:18-19 the warning is given, **"Pride goeth before destruction, and an haughty spirit before a fall. Better it is to be of an humble spirit with the lowly, than to divide the spoil with the proud."** As we have previously noted, the spirit of pride will keep us from spiritual revival and will lead us to spiritual destruction. In addition, the spirit of pride will remove us from the path of spiritual revival and will cause us to fall into selfishness and sin. Therefore, in the realm of spiritual revival, it is far better to be of a humble spirit with the lowly and unrecognized, than it is to receive some portion of men's praise and honor with the proud.

When we have entered into and are walking on the path of spiritual revival, we must heed the warning of 1 Corinthians 10:12-13 – *"Wherefore let him that thinketh he standeth take heed lest he fall. There hath no temptation taken you but such as is common to man: but God is faithful, who will not suffer you to be tempted above that ye are able; but will with the temptation also make a way to escape, that ye may be able to bear it."* We must ever remember that we do not stand in the way of spiritual revival by our own strength and ability, but by the sufficiency of God's grace. We must never forget that in the weakness of our sinful flesh, we can fall and be overcome by any temptation that has overtaken our fellow men. Yea, we must ever remember that the way of spiritual revival does not erase the reality of temptation, but that we will indeed face temptation to sin all along the way. Yea, we must never forget that our only way to bear up under temptation with victory is through utter dependence upon our Lord God's empowering grace and everlasting faithfulness.

We must ever remember that *"though we walk in the flesh, we do not war after the flesh."* (2 Corinthians 10:3) We must never forget that *"the weapons of our* [spiritual] *warfare are not carnal, but mighty through God to the pulling down of* [spiritual] *strong holds."* (2 Corinthians 10:4) Therefore, through utter dependence upon our Lord God's all-sufficient grace, we must cast down all carnal imaginations *"and every high thing that exalteth itself against the knowledge of God,"* and must bring *"into captivity every thought to the obedience of Christ."* (2 Corinthians 10:5) At any time, to pursue the abundant, victorious, fruitful Christian life in self-dependence is to destroy spiritual revival in our lives.

Furthermore, as we serve in ministry through spiritual revival, we must heed the warning of Romans 12:3 – *"For I say, through the grace given unto me, to every man that is among you, not to think of himself more highly than he ought to think; but to think soberly, according as God hath dealt to every man the measure of faith."* We must ever remember that we are saved from our sin and able to serve in the ministry only by God's grace. (1 Corinthians 15:10) Therefore, we must never think of ourselves more highly than others, but must think soberly of ourselves as the lowly servants of the Lord, humbly and faithfully fulfilling the ministry responsibility that He has given us by His grace.

"For we dare not make ourselves of the number, or compare ourselves with some that commend themselves: but they measuring themselves by themselves, and comparing themselves among themselves, are not wise." (2 Corinthians 10:12) *"For if a man think himself to be something, when he is nothing, he deceiveth himself."* If we desire to remain on the path of spiritual revival, we *dare not* compare ourselves with others in order to commend ourselves above others. Measuring ourselves by others and comparing ourselves among others is spiritual foolishness and self-deception. Our standard for spiritual maturity and ministry is not established by others' lives, but by God's Word. At any time, to think more highly of ourselves than others is to destroy spiritual revival in our lives.

Finally, as we relate to others through spiritual revival, we must heed the warning and instruction of Philippians 2:3-4 – *"Let nothing be done through strife or vainglory; but in lowliness of mind let each esteem other better than themselves. Look not every man on his own things, but every man also on the things of others."* We must ever remember that the strife and vainglory of selfishness and pride is spiritually contrary to the Spirit-filled walk of revival living. Thus Galatians 5:25-26 declares, *"If we live in the Spirit, let us also walk in the Spirit. Let us not be desirous of vain glory, provoking one another, envying one another."*

Yea, we must never forget that true, Spirit-filled love in our relationships with others is longsuffering and kind, does not envy, does not exalt itself, is not puffed up with the spirit of pride, does not behave itself in an inappropriate manner, does not selfishly seek its own, is not easily provoked, and does not have an evil attitude against others. (1 Corinthians 13:4-5) At any time, to walk in the strife, vainglory, and bad attitude of selfishness and pride is to destroy spiritual revival in our lives.

On the one hand, where there is true spiritual revival, a proud spirit is reproved and purged away. On the other hand, where there is a spirit of pride, spiritual revival is prevented or removed away.

Chapter Ten

God Giveth Grace unto the Humble

In the previous chapter, we focused our attention upon the Biblical truth that the Lord our God does not revive, restore, or renew the proud, but resists the proud. Yet the Lord our God does indeed promise *"to revive the spirit of the humble, and to revive the heart of the contrite ones."* (Isaiah 57:15) He promises to pour out His reviving, restoring, and renewing grace upon the humble. *"But he giveth more grace. Wherefore he saith, God resisteth the proud, but giveth grace unto the humble."* (James 4:6)

The Lord's Favor upon the Humble

The spirit of humility is that which the Lord our God respects and honors. Psalm 138:6 proclaims, *"Though the LORD be high, yet hath he respect unto the lowly: but the proud he knoweth afar off."* He is the high and lofty One. He is the most high God. He is infinitely high above all the creation. Even *"the heaven and heaven of heavens cannot contain Him."* (2 Chronicles 2:6) Indeed, He is so high above all that He must humble Himself in condescension just to *"behold the things that are in heaven, and in the earth!"* (Psalm 113:4-6) Yet the most high God has respect unto those of a lowly and humble spirit. In the closing portion of Isaiah 66:2, He declares, *"But to this man will I look, even to him that is poor and of a contrite spirit, and trembleth at my word."*

➢ His Ear Is Open unto Their Cry

The infinitely high and lofty One looks with favor upon the humble, and in His favor He pours out the abundance of His grace upon them. In the abundance of His grace, His ear is open unto the cry of their prayer. Speaking as one of the lowly, David gave report in the opening half of Psalm 138:3, ***"In the day when I cried thou answeredst me."*** Again the closing portion of Psalm 9:12 states, ***"He forgetteth not the cry of the humble."*** Yet again Psalm 10:17 gives assurance, saying, ***"LORD, thou hast heard the desire of the humble: thou wilt prepare their heart, thou wilt cause thine ear to hear."*** As the humble cry out in prayer for spiritual revival, the Lord our God graciously hears and pours out His gracious work of spiritual revival upon their hearts and lives.

➢ He Grants Strength unto Their Soul

In the abundance of His grace, the Lord our God also grants spiritual strength unto the soul of the humble. Speaking as one of the lowly, David continued in Psalm 138:3, ***"In the day when I cried thou answeredst me, and strengthenedst me with strength in my soul."*** Even so, Psalm 27:14 gives the instruction and promise, ***"Wait on the LORD: be of good courage, and he shall strengthen thine heart: wait, I say, on the LORD."***

Again in Isaiah 40:31 the promise is given, ***"But they that wait upon the LORD shall renew their strength; they shall mount up with wings as eagles; they shall run, and not be weary; and they shall walk, and not faint."*** As we humbly wait upon Him, He will renew the failing strength of our hearts with the almighty strength of His hand. Then we will be able to mount up with the wings of spiritual revival. Then we will be able to run in spiritual revival without becoming weary in well doing and will be able to walk in spiritual revival without fainting in our minds.

Yet again in 2 Corinthians 12:7-9 the apostle Paul gave report, saying, ***"And lest I should be exalted above measure through the abundance of the revelations, there was given to me a thorn in the flesh, the messenger of Satan to buffet me, lest I should be*** *exalted above measure. For this thing I besought the Lord thrice, that it might depart from me. And he said unto me, My grace is sufficient for thee: for my strength is made perfect in weakness. Most gladly therefore will I rather glory in my infirmities, that the power of Christ may rest upon me."* When we will humbly acknowledge our utter weakness and wholly depend upon our Lord's grace, then we will find the power of Christ for spiritual revival resting upon us. Then we will find His grace sufficient for us and His strength perfected in us.

➢ **He Renews Their Inner Man in Trouble**

In the abundance of His grace, the Lord our God also renews the inner man of the humble in times of trouble. Speaking as one of the lowly, David expressed the assurance in the opening portion of Psalm 138:7, *"Though I walk in the midst of trouble, thou wilt revive me."* Again Psalm 147:3 declares, *"He healeth the broken in heart, and bindeth up their wounds."* Yet again in 2 Corinthians 4:15-16 the apostle Paul gave report, saying, *"For all things are for your sakes, that the abundant grace might through the thanksgiving of many redound to the glory of God. For which cause we faint not; but though our outward man perish, yet the inward man is renewed day by day."* Yes, in this world we shall experience much tribulation and trouble. Yet if we will depend upon the Lord with a humble spirit, He will bind up the wounds of our heart and will renew the strength of our inner man from day to day.

➢ **He Delivers Them from Their Enemies**

In the abundance of His grace, the Lord our God also delivers the humble from the power of their enemies – especially from the power of their spiritual enemies. Speaking as one of the lowly, David continued in the closing portion of Psalm 138:7, *"Thou shalt stretch forth thine hand against the wrath of mine enemies, and thy right hand shall save me."* Again in Psalm 34:17-19 the assurance is given, *"The righteous cry, and the LORD heareth, and delivereth them out of all their troubles. The LORD is nigh unto them that are of a broken heart; and saveth such as be of a contrite spirit. Many are the afflictions of the righteous: but the LORD delivereth him out of them all."* Yet again James 4:7 gives the instruction and promise, *"Submit yourselves therefore to God. Resist the devil, and he will flee from you."* As the servants of the Lord, our primary enemies are not physical, but spiritual. Yet if we will submit ourselves unto the Lord with a contrite spirit, He will deliver us from the attacks and afflictions of our spiritual enemies. Furthermore, in the midst spiritual conflict, He will so empower us that we may victoriously withstand the devil's attacks until he flees *from us*.

➢ He Guides Them in the Right Way

In the abundance of His grace, the Lord our God also guides the humble in the way of righteousness. Psalm 25:9 proclaims, *"The meek will he guide in judgment: and the meek will he teach his way."* Again in Psalm 32:8 the Lord our God declares, *"I will instruct thee and teach thee in the way which thou shalt go: I will guide thee with mine eye."* Yet again Proverbs 3:5-6 gives the instruction and promise, *"Trust in the LORD with all thine heart; and lean not unto thine own understanding. In all thy ways acknowledge him, and he shall direct thy paths."* When we will humbly deny the value of our own understanding, and will humbly trust in the Lord with all our heart, and will humbly acknowledge the Lord in all our ways, then He will teach us His perfect way and will guide us with His loving eye. Then He will direct our paths in wisdom and righteousness.

➢ He Empowers Them unto Fruitfulness

In the abundance of His grace, the Lord our God also empowers the humble unto spiritual fruitfulness. In John 15:5 our Lord Jesus Christ revealed the truth and the promise, *"I am the vine, ye are the branches. He that abideth in me, and I in him, the same bringeth forth much fruit: for without me ye can do nothing."* Again in 1 Corinthians 15:10 the apostle Paul gave the testimony, *"But by the grace of God I am what I am: and his grace which was bestowed upon me was not in vain; but I laboured more abundantly than they all: yet not I, but the grace of God which was with me."* Yet again 2 Corinthians 9:8 gives the assurance, *"And God is able to make all grace abound toward you; that ye, always having all sufficiency in all things, may abound to every good work.*" When we will humbly abide in Christ, and allow Him to abide in us, He will make all grace abound toward us, so that we may have all spiritual sufficiency to abound unto every good and to bring forth much spiritual fruit, all for the glory of His name.

➤ He Fills Them with Joy and Peace

In the abundance of His grace, the Lord our God also fills the humble with joy, peace, and satisfaction in Him. Isaiah 29:19 proclaims, *"The meek also shall increase their joy in the LORD, and the poor among men shall rejoice in the Holy One of Israel."* Again in Matthew 11:29 our Lord Jesus Christ gave the instruction and promise, *"Take my yoke upon you, and learn of me; for I am meek and lowly in heart: and ye shall find rest unto your souls."* Yet again in Psalm 22:26 the assurance is given, *"The meek shall eat and be satisfied: they shall praise the LORD that seek him: your heart shall live for ever."* When we will willingly take our Lord's yoke of submission upon ourselves and will learn of Him to be meek in spirit and humble in heart, then we shall find perfect rest unto our souls, increase our joy in the Lord, and be satisfied with the pleasures of our Lord's fellowship.

➤ He Shall Exalt Them unto Blessing

Finally, in the abundance of His grace, the Lord our God shall exalt the humble unto the place of blessing. Psalm 147:6 reports, *"The LORD lifteth up the meek: he casteth the wicked down to the ground."* Again Psalm 37:11 gives promise, *"But the meek shall inherit the earth; and shall delight themselves in the abundance of peace."* Yet again Psalm 149:4 declares, *"For the LORD taketh pleasure in his people: he will beautify the meek with salvation."* Even so, 1 Peter 5:6 gives the instruction and promise, *"Humble yourselves therefore under the mighty hand of God, that he may exalt you in due time."*

The Biblical Instruction to Humility

In Micah 6:6-7 the question is asked, *"Wherewith shall I come before the LORD, and bow myself before the high God? Shall I come before him with burnt offerings, with calves of a year old?*

Will the LORD be pleased with thousands of rams, or with ten thousands of rivers of oil? Shall I give my firstborn for my transgression, the fruit of my body for the sin of my soul?" Then in verse 8 the answer is revealed, *"He hath shewed thee, O man, what is good; and what doth the LORD require of thee, but to do justly, and to love mercy, and to walk humbly with thy God?"* This is the only way that we will ever enter and continue upon the path of spiritual revival. We must humble ourselves before the Lord our God and walk humbly in fellowship with Him.

By its very nature, the path of spiritual revival requires that we walk in the fear of the Lord; and humility before the Lord is an essential ingredient to the fear of the Lord. The opening half of Proverbs 8:13 states, *"The fear of the LORD is to hate evil;"* and the opening half of Proverbs 14:2 adds, *"He that walketh in his uprightness feareth the LORD."* This rejection of evil and this walk in uprightness are the characteristics of spiritual revival, and they are founded upon the fear of the Lord. Even so, Proverbs 22:4 inseparably joins the spirit of humility and the fear of the Lord, saying, *"By humility and the fear of the LORD are riches, and honour, and life."* Only by the spirit of humility and the fear of the Lord can we find the spiritual riches, divine honor, and abundant life of spiritual revival.

To walk in spiritual revival is to walk in spiritual fellowship with the Lord our God. Thus by its very nature, the path of spiritual revival requires that we humbly take our Lord's yoke of submission and service upon us, and that we humbly learn of Him. Yea, by its very nature, the path of spiritual revival requires that we learn *from* our Lord Jesus Christ to walk *as* our Lord Jesus Christ – "meek and lowly in heart." Even so, in Matthew 11:29 He declared, *"Take my yoke upon you, and learn of me; for I am meek and lowly in heart: and ye shall find rest unto your souls."*

By its very nature, the path of spiritual revival requires that we deny ourselves, daily take up our cross of self-sacrifice, and humbly follow our Lord in every step of our lives. (Luke 9:23) Yea, by its very nature, the path of spiritual revival requires that we walk with the same humble mindset as our Lord Jesus Christ. *"Let this mind be in you, which was also in Christ Jesus: who, being in the form of God, thought it not robbery to be equal with God: but made himself of no reputation, and took upon him the form of a servant, and was made in the likeness of men: and being found in fashion as a man, he humbled himself, and became obedient unto death, even the death of the cross."* (Philippians 2:5-8)

By its very nature, the path of spiritual revival requires that we humbly minister unto others with the servant's heart of our Lord. In John 13:13-16 He gave instruction, saying, *"Ye call me Master and Lord: and ye say well; for so I am. If I then, your Lord and Master, have washed your feet; ye also ought to wash one another's feet. For I have given you an example, that ye should do as I have done to you. Verily, verily, I say unto you, The servant is not greater than his lord; neither he that is sent greater than he that sent him. If ye know these things, happy are ye if ye do them."*

By its very nature, the path of spiritual revival requires that we maintain a spirit of humility in all our conduct with others. In Ephesians 4:1-3 the instruction is given, *"I therefore, the prisoner of the Lord, beseech you that ye walk worthy of the vocation wherewith ye are called, with all lowliness and meekness, with longsuffering, forbearing one another in love; endeavoring to keep the unity of the spirit in the bond of peace."* Again in Philippians 2:3-4 the instruction is given, *"Let nothing be done through strife or vainglory; but in lowliness of mind let each esteem other better than themselves. Look not every man on his own things, but every man also on the things of others."*

Yet again in Titus 3:1-2 the instruction is given, *"Put them in mind to be subject to principalities and powers, to obey magistrates, to be ready to every good work, to speak evil of no man, to be no brawlers, but gentle, shewing all meekness unto all men."* Finally, in 1 Peter 5:5 the instruction is given, *"Likewise, ye younger, submit yourselves unto the elder. Yea, all of you be subject one to another, and be clothed with humility: for God resisteth the proud, and giveth grace to the humble."*

Only when we will humble ourselves like a little child before our Lord, shall we find the greatness of His revival work in our hearts. (Matthew 18:4) *"LORD, my heart is not haughty, nor mine eyes lofty: neither do I exercise myself in great matters, or in things too high for me. Surely I have behaved and quieted myself, as a child that is weaned of his mother: my soul is even as a weaned child."* (Psalm 131:1-2)

Only when we will be of a poor and contrite spirit, trembling at our Lord's Word, shall He appear unto our joy, favoring us with His reviving fellowship. (Isaiah 66:2, 5) Only when we will seek for our Lord to increase with preeminence in all things, even as we decrease, shall the power of spiritual revival fill and flow through our lives. (John 3:30)

Before our Lord will graciously honor us with the blessings of spiritual revival, we must humble ourselves in His sight. *"The fear of the LORD is the instruction of wisdom; and before honour is humility."* (Proverbs 15:33)

2 Chronicles 7:12-14

And the LORD appeared to Solomon by night,
and said unto him,
I have heard thy prayer,
and have chosen this place to myself
for an house of sacrifice.
If I shut up heaven that there be no rain,
or if I command the locusts to devour the land,
or if I send pestilence among my people;
if my people, which are called by my name,
shall humble themselves,
and pray,
and seek my face,
and turn from their wicked ways;
then will I hear from heaven,
and will forgive their sin,
and will heal their land.

Chapter Eleven

If My People

2 Chronicles 7:14 is a commonly recognized verse concerning the relationship of humility and spiritual revival. There the Lord our God declared unto King Solomon, *"If my people, which are called by my name, shall humble themselves, and pray, and seek my face, and turn from their wicked ways; then will I hear from heaven, and will forgive their sin, and will heal their land."*

Yet many have contended that it is not contextually appropriate to apply the message of this verse unto believers today. They contend that when it is viewed within its Old Testament context, it has strict application to the land of God's chosen nation Israel, and no application to the lives of New Testament believers. However, when we understand the message of this verse *within* its context, we find that the principle of this passage has both an appropriate and spiritually powerful application to our present day. What then is the context of this passage?

Solomon's Building of the Temple

The context of 2 Chronicles 7:14 specifically relates to Solomon's building and dedication of the temple in Jerusalem. King David, Solomon's father, had desired to build a temple house for the name of the Lord. Yet the Lord had forbidden him from doing so because the Lord had chosen him to be a warrior king, and as such his hands had shed blood. (1 Chronicles 17:1-4; 28:2-3) Rather, the Lord chose David's son Solomon to sit upon the throne as king after David and to build the temple house for His name. (1 Chronicles 17:11-14; 28:4-7)

Even so, in 2 Chronicles 2:1 we read, *"And Solomon determined to build an house for the name of the LORD, and an house for his kingdom."* Furthermore, in 2 Chronicles 3:1-2 we read, *"Then Solomon began to build the house of the LORD at Jerusalem in mount Moriah, where the LORD appeared unto David his father, in the place that David had prepared in the threshingfloor of Ornan the Jebusite. And he began to build in the second day of the second month, in the fourth year of his reign."*

Finally, in 2 Chronicles 5:1 we read, *"Thus all the work that Solomon made for the house of the LORD was finished: and Solomon brought in all the things that David his father had dedicated; and the silver, and the gold, and all the instruments, put he among the treasures of the house of God."*

Solomon's Dedication of the Temple

2 Chronicles 5:2-3 continues, *"Then Solomon assembled the elders of Israel, and all the heads of the tribes, the chief of the fathers of the children of Israel, unto Jerusalem, to bring up the ark of the covenant of the LORD out of the city of David, which is Zion. Wherefore all the men of Israel assembled themselves unto the king in the feast which was in the seventh month."* This was the Feast of Tabernacles, an eight-day holiday of thanksgiving for the harvest. (Leviticus 23:33-43; Numbers 29:12-38)

At that time the Levites *"brought up the ark, and the tabernacle of the congregation, and all the holy vessels that were in the tabernacle."* (2 Chronicles 5:5) *"Also king Solomon, and all the congregation of Israel that were assembled unto him before the ark, sacrificed sheep and oxen, which could not be told nor numbered for multitude. And the priests brought in the ark of the covenant of the LORD unto his place, to the oracle of the house, into the most holy place, even under the wings of the cherubims."* (2 Chronicles 5:6-7)

Then, as the priests came out of the holy place, the trumpeters, singers, and musicians lifted up praise unto the Lord. *"It came even to pass, as the trumpeters and singers were as one, to make one sound to be heard in praising and thanking the LORD; and when they lifted up their voice with the trumpets and cymbals and instruments of musick, and praised the LORD, saying, For he is good; for his mercy endureth for ever: that then the house was filled with a cloud, even the house of the LORD; so that the priests could not stand to minister by reason of the cloud: for the glory of the LORD had filled the house of God."* (2 Chronicles 5:13-14)

"Then said Solomon, The LORD hath said that he would dwell in the thick darkness. But I have built an house of habitation for thee, and a place for thy dwelling for ever. And the king turned his face, and blessed the whole congregation of Israel: and all the congregation of Israel stood." (2 Chronicles 6:1-3) Furthermore, Solomon publicly blessed the Lord God of Israel for having fulfilled His promise unto David. (2 Chronicles 6:4-11)

Then King Solomon *"stood before the altar of the LORD in the presence of all the congregation of Israel"* upon *"a brasen scaffold, of five cubits long, and five cubits broad, and three cubits high."* (2 Chronicles 6:12-13) *"And upon it he stood, and kneeled down upon his knees before all the congregation of Israel, and spread forth his hands toward heaven."* (2 Chronicles 6:13) On his knees before the people, Solomon lifted up a prayer to the Lord concerning the temple, which extends from 2 Chronicles 6:14-42.

"Now when Solomon had made an end of praying, the fire came down from heaven, and consumed the burnt offering and the sacrifices; and the glory of the LORD filled the house. And the priests could not enter into the house of the LORD, because the glory of the LORD had filled the LORD'S house. And when all the children of Israel saw how the fire came down, and the glory of the LORD upon the house, they bowed themselves with their faces to the ground upon the pavement, and worshipped, and praised the LORD, saying, For he is good; for his mercy endureth for ever." (2 Chronicles 7:1-3)

"Then the king and all the people offered sacrifices before the LORD." (2 Chronicles 7:4) King Solomon himself offered a sacrificed of 22,000 oxen and 120,000 sheep. *"So the king and all the people dedicated the house of God."* (2 Chronicles 7:5) Also at the same time, Solomon and all Israel with him kept the Feast of Tabernacles. (2 Chronicles 7:8-10) *"Thus Solomon finished the house of the LORD, and the king's house: and all that came into Solomon's heart to make in the house of the LORD, and in his own house, he prosperously effected."* (2 Chronicles 7:11)

Solomon's Prayer concerning the Temple

Yet as we consider the context of 2 Chronicles 7:12-14, we must look more closely at Solomon's prayer in 2 Chronicles 6:14-42. In 2 Chronicles 7:12 we read, *"And the LORD appeared to Solomon by night, and said unto him, I have heard thy prayer, and have chosen this place to myself for an house of sacrifice."* Thus we understand that our Lord's message in 2 Chronicles 7:12-14 was delivered in direct response to Solomon's *prayer*.

In 2 Chronicles 6:14-15 Solomon began his prayer with praise unto the Lord for His faithfulness and mercy – *"And said, O LORD God of Israel, there is no God like thee in the heaven, nor in the earth; which keepest covenant, and shewest mercy unto thy servants, that walk before thee with all their hearts: thou which hast kept with thy servant David my father that which thou hast promised him; and spakest with thy mouth, and hast fulfilled it with thine hand, as it is this day."* In verses 16-17 Solomon prayed that the Lord might remain faithful in fulfilling His promise to David.

Yet in verse 18 Solomon expressed his recognition that the Lord's presence cannot actually be contained within a temple building – *"But will God in very deed dwell with men on the earth? Behold, heaven and the heaven of heavens cannot contain thee; how much less this house which I have built!"* Therefore, Solomon made request in verses 19-21 that the Lord's eyes might be open upon the temple day and night, in order that He might hearken from His dwelling place in heaven unto the prayers and supplications of His people that they would make toward His temple.

Even so, in the closing portion of verse 21, Solomon prayed, *"Hear thou from thy dwelling place, even from heaven; and when thou hearest, forgive."* Herein we learn that Solomon was not primarily focused on the prayers of God's people for material things. Rather, Solomon was primarily focused on the prayers of God's people for forgiveness of sin, removal of chastening, and restoration to fellowship. In fact, throughout verses 22-39 Solomon presented seven scenarios in which people might pray in or toward the temple of God; and of those seven scenarios, four of them concern God's people under the chastening hand of the Lord, crying out in repentance for forgiveness and restoration.

Then in verses 40-42 Solomon ended his prayer, saying, *"Now, my God, let, I beseech thee, thine eyes be open, and let thine ears be attent unto the prayer that is made in this place. Now therefore arise, O LORD God, into thy resting place, thou, and the ark of thy strength: let thy priests, O LORD God, be clothed with salvation, and let thy saints rejoice in goodness."*

The Lord's Response to Solomon's Prayer

Since the Lord's message in 2 Chronicles 7:12-14 was delivered in direct response to Solomon's prayer, it is necessary for us to focus our attention upon those parts of Solomon's prayer unto which the Lord specifically responded.

➢ **A Focus upon the People of God**

In 2 Chronicles 7:14 the Lord focused His response upon His relationship with His own people, saying, *"If my people, which are called by my name."* Of the seven prayer scenarios that Solomon included in his prayer, six of them concern the prayers of God's chosen people Israel; whereas one of them concerns the prayers of foreigners.

The one scenario concerning foreigners is found in verses 32-33 – *"Moreover concerning the stranger, which is not of thy people Israel, but is come from a far country for thy great name's sake, and thy mighty hand, and thy stretched out arm; if they come and pray in this house; then hear thou from the heavens, even from thy dwelling place, and do according to all that the stranger calleth to thee for; that all people of the earth may know thy name, and fear thee, as doth thy people Israel, and may know that this house which I have built is called by thy name."*

> ➤ **A Focus upon the Sin of God's People**

Also in 2 Chronicles 7:14 the Lord focused His response upon the sinful ways of His people and upon their need to repent of that sin, saying, *"If my people, which are called by my name, shall humble themselves, and pray, and seek my face, and turn from their wicked ways."* Of the six prayer scenarios in Solomon's prayer that concern God's people, five of them concern the sinful ways of God's people; and of those five scenarios, four of them specifically mention the repentance of God's people.

The first scenario is found in verses 22-23 – *"If a man sin against his neighbour, and an oath be laid upon him to make him swear, and the oath come before thine altar in this house; then hear thou from heaven, and do, and judge thy servants, by requiting the wicked, by recompensing his way upon his own head; and by justifying the righteous, by giving him according to his righteousness."* This scenario concerns the sin of an Israelite against his neighbor and the desire for the Lord to bring forth justice. This scenario is the one that does not specifically mention the matter of repentance.

The second scenario is found in verses 24-25 and concerns both the sin and repentance of God's people. Verses 24 states, *"And if thy people Israel be put to the worse before the enemy, because they have sinned against thee; and shall return and confess thy name, and pray and make supplication before thee in this house."*

The third scenario is found in verses 26-27 and also concerns both the sin and repentance of God's people. Verse 26 states, *"When the heaven is shut up, and there is no rain, because they have sinned against thee; yet if they pray toward this place, and confess thy name, and turn from their sin, when thou dost afflict them."*

The fourth scenario is found in verses 28-31 and also concerns both the sinful ways and repentant supplication of God's people. Verses 29-30 state, *"Then what prayer or what supplication soever shall be made of any man, or of all thy people Israel, when every one shall know his own sore and his own grief, and shall spread forth his hands in this house: then hear thou from heaven thy dwelling place, and forgive, and render unto every man according unto all his ways, whose heart thou knowest; (for thou only knowest the hearts of the children of men)."*

The fifth scenario is found in verses 32-33 and is the one that concerns the prayers of foreigners. Then the sixth scenario is found in verses 34-35 and does not concern the sinful ways of God's people. Rather, it concerns the prayer of God's people for the Lord to maintain their cause when they go out to war against their enemies by the way in which the Lord Himself would send them.

Yet this sixth scenario very quickly shifts into the seventh scenario of verses 36-39. This last scenario concerns the Lord's delivering of His people into the hand of their enemies because of their sinful ways and concerns their repentance of those sinful ways. Verses 36-38 state, *"If they sin against thee, (for there is no man which sinneth not,) and thou be angry with them, and deliver them over before their enemies, and they carry them away captives unto a land far off or near; yet if they bethink themselves in the land whither they are carried captive, and turn and pray unto thee in the land of their captivity, saying, We have sinned, we have done amiss, and have dealt wickedly; if they return to thee with all their heart and with all their soul in the land of their captivity, whither they have carried them captives, and pray toward their land, which thou gavest unto their fathers, and toward the city which thou hast chosen, and toward the house which I have built for thy name."*

➤ A Focus upon the Chastening of the Lord

In 2 Chronicles 7:13 the Lord focused His response upon His work of chastening in the lives of His people, saying, *"If I shut up heaven that there be no rain, or if I command the locusts to devour the land, or if I send pestilence among my people."* Herein the Lord does not refer to these things simply as circumstantial troubles. Rather, He refers to these things as troubles that He Himself might bring upon the lives of His people. But why would the Lord our God bring such troubles upon His own people?

In two scenarios of Solomon's prayer, he mentioned the possible defeat of God's people at the hand of their enemies. The opening portion of verse 24 states, *"And if thy people Israel be put to the worse before the enemy, because they have sinned against thee."* Again verse 36 states, *"If they sin against thee, (for there is no man which sinneth not,) and thou be angry with them, and deliver them over before their enemies, and they carry them away captives unto a land far off or near."* In both scenarios their defeat is presented as the Lord's chastening for their sin.

Furthermore, in two other scenarios, Solomon mentioned the possible trouble of God's people with drought and pestilence. The opening portion of verse 26 states, *"When the heaven is shut up, and there is no rain, because they have sinned against thee."* Again verse 28 states, *"If there be dearth in the land, if there be pestilence, if there be blasting, or mildew, locusts, or caterpillers; if their enemies besiege them in the cities of their land; whatsoever sore or whatsoever sickness there be."* Again the drought and pestilence is presented as the Lord's chastening for their sin.

Thus in 2 Chronicles 7:13 the focus is not to be upon the details of the troubles that the Lord might send. Rather, the focus is to be upon *the purpose* for those troubles. The focus is not to be upon the shutting up of the rain, or upon the devouring of the land, or upon the pestilence among the people. Rather, the focus is to be upon *the principle* that the Lord our God chastens His people for their sinful ways. This principle was true for God's people in the time of the Old Testament, and this principle remains truth for God's people in this time of the New Testament.

Even so, in the New Testament passage of Hebrews 12:5-8, God's Word declares, *"And ye have forgotten the exhortation which speaketh unto you as unto children, My son, despise not thou the chastening of the Lord, nor faint when thou art rebuked of him: for whom the Lord loveth he chasteneth, and scourgeth every son whom he receiveth. If ye endure chastening, God dealeth with you as with sons; for what son is he whom the father chasteneth not? But if ye be without chastisement, whereof all are partakers, then are ye bastards, and not sons."*

➢ **A Focus upon the Forgiveness of the Lord**

Finally, in the closing portion of 2 Chronicles 7:14, the Lord focused His response upon His forgiveness and restoration for His repentant people, saying, *"Then will I hear from heaven, and will forgive their sin, and will heal their land."*

In 2 Chronicles 6:25, concerning those among God's people who would return in confession unto the Lord and make supplication before the Lord, Solomon prayed, *"Then hear thou from the heavens, and forgive the sin of thy people Israel, and bring them again unto the land which thou gavest to them and to their fathers."* Again in verse 27, concerning those who would pray unto the Lord, confess His holy name, and turn from their sin, Solomon prayed, *"Then hear thou from heaven, and forgive the sin of thy servants, and of thy people Israel, when thou hast taught them the good way, wherein they should walk; and send rain upon thy land, which thou hast given unto thy people for an inheritance."*

Yet again in verses 30-31 Solomon prayed, *"Then hear thou from heaven thy dwelling place, and forgive, and render unto every man according unto all his ways, whose heart thou knowest; (for thou only knowest the hearts of the children of men:) that they may fear thee, to walk in thy ways, so long as they live in the land which thou gavest unto our fathers."* Finally, in verse 39, concerning those who would pray in confession of their sin and return unto the Lord with all their heart and soul, Solomon prayed, *"Then hear thou from the heavens, even from thy dwelling place, their prayer and their supplications, and maintain their cause, and forgive thy people which have sinned against thee."*

Therefore, within its context the principle of our Lord's message in 2 Chronicles 7:12-14 has application to the people of God who are under the chastening hand of the Lord our God because of their sinful ways. The drought, devoured land, and pestilence simply represent our Lord's hand of chastening against His people. Furthermore, this passage is our Lord's call unto His chastened people to humble themselves in repentance of sin and in returning to Him. Finally, this passage is our Lord's promise unto His repentant people that He will forgive their sin, remove His hand of chastening from them, and restore them to the blessing of His favor, where the healing of the land simply represents the removal of chastening and the restoration to favor.

Chapter Twelve

If I Send Pestilence among My People

In 2 Chronicles 7:13-14 the Lord our God presented a lengthy sentence that includes two different series of conditions and a series of promises. Verse 13 presents a series of three conditional statements concerning the chastening of our Lord against His sinning people. Furthermore, the opening portion of verse 14 presents a series of four conditions concerning the call of our Lord unto His chastened people. Thereby our Lord calls for His people to repent of their sinful ways. Finally, the closing portion of verse 14 presents a series of three promises concerning the commitment of our Lord unto His repentant people.

In 2 Chronicles 7:13 our Lord presented three possible cases by which He Himself might bring His own hand against His people. There He stated, *"**If I shut up heaven that there be no rain, or if I command the locusts to devour the land, or if I send pestilence among my people.**"* As we have learned previously, each of these three cases is directly connected to Solomon's prayer concerning the temple in 2 Chronicles 6:14-42.

In the opening portion of 2 Chronicles 6:26, Solomon presented the following scenario in his prayer, *"**When the heaven is shut up, and there is no rain, because they have sinned against thee.**"* Again in verse 28 he presented the scenario, *"**If there be dearth in the land, if there be pestilence, if there be blasting, or mildew, locusts, or caterpillers; if their enemies besiege them in the cities**"* *of their land; whatsoever sore or whatsoever sickness there be."* In his prayer Solomon indicated that these possible scenarios might come against God's people specifically *because they had sinned against the Lord*. Thus we understand that the principle truth of our Lord's message in 2 Chronicles 7:13 concerns our Lord's hand of chastening against His sinning people.

The Certainty of Chastening

Even so, in Hebrews 12:5-8 God's Word speaks to the New Testament believer, saying, *"And ye have forgotten the exhortation which speaketh unto you as unto children, My son, despise not thou the chastening of the Lord, nor faint when thou art rebuked of him: for whom the Lord loveth he chasteneth, and scourgeth every son whom he receiveth. If ye endure chastening, God dealeth with you as with sons; for what son is he whom the father chasteneth not? But if ye be without chastisement, whereof all are partakers, then are ye bastards, and not sons."*

Hebrews 12:5-8 speaks concerning the spiritual parent-child relationship of every born again child of God with God their heavenly Father. It speaks unto us "as unto children." In so doing, this passage reveals that our Lord's hand of chastening is a certainty in the lives of every single child of God. When we sin against the Lord our God and heavenly Father, He *will* rebuke us, chasten us, and even scourge us until we repent of our sins and return unto Him. In fact, Hebrews 12:6-8 presents a three-fold foundation for the certainty of our Lord's chastening in our lives.

First, spiritual chastening from our Lord's hand is certain because it is a reality of our Lord's love for His children. The Lord our God and heavenly Father delights in His dear children. As such a loving Father, He corrects His dear children faithfully from any unrighteous way. *"For whom the LORD loveth he correcteth; even as a father the son in whom he delighteth."* (Proverbs 3:12) He will not withhold chastening from His dear children, and thereby demonstrate an unloving disregard for their character and conduct. (Proverbs 13:24) Rather, out of love for His children, our Lord promptly chastens them of anything that will do spiritual damage to their lives.

Second, spiritual chastening from our Lord's hand is certain because it is a universal principle of our Lord's relationship with His children. The closing portion of Hebrews 12:6 teaches us that the Lord our God and heavenly Father *"**scourgeth every son whom he receiveth.**"* Every child of God experiences the corrective work of God our heavenly Father. Not a single child of God is excluded from the chastening hand of the Father, either through privilege or neglect. Whenever any of us who are the children of God walks in disobedience and sin against Him, our heavenly Father rebukes us, chastens us, and even scourges us until we come to repentance.

Third, spiritual chastening from our Lord's hand is certain because it is an evidence of our sonship in God's family. Hebrews 12:7-8 declares, *"**If ye endure chastening, God dealeth with you as with sons; for what son is he whom the father chasteneth not? But if ye be without chastisement, whereof all are partakers, then are ye bastards, and not sons.**"* If we experience the Lord's chastening hand when we are in disobedience and sin, then the Lord our God is dealing with us "as with sons." Such chastening is an evidence that the Lord our God has indeed received us as a dear child in His spiritual family. However, if we do not experience such chastisement from the Father's hand, then it is because we are not actually one of His dear children. Since *all* of the Father's children are partakers of chastisement, then an individual "without chastisement" must not truly be one of the Father's children.

The Character of Chastening

The details of our Lord's chastening hand will vary in each case. He will employ that which will be most appropriate and effective in each believer's life. In 2 Chronicles 7:13 our Lord presents three examples of chastening that He might send against His people Israel. This list is not an exhaustive list, for many other forms of chastening are revealed throughout the Word of God. Yet these three examples may be viewed as suggestive and illustrative concerning the character of our Lord's chastening hand in our lives.

➢ Our Fellowship with the Lord Will Be Broken

The first characteristic of our Lord's chastening hand will *always* be that our spiritual fellowship with Him will be broken. The first possible case of chastening against His people Israel that our Lord presented in 2 Chronicles 7:13 was, *"If I shut up heaven that there be no rain."* Quite literally our Lord was speaking of bringing a drought against His people Israel. Yet this is also suggestive and illustrative of our Lord's shutting up from us the high and holy place of His blessed fellowship.

Isaiah 59:1-2 declares, *"Behold, the LORD'S hand is not shortened, that it cannot save; neither his ear heavy, that it cannot hear: but your iniquities have separated between you and your God, and your sins have hid his face from you, that he will not hear."* Our iniquities separate between us and our God. They serve as a great spiritual barrier that divides us from the fellowship of our Lord. Our sins hide His face from us. They turn away from us His gracious gaze of fellowship and favor. They turn against us His fierce gaze of anger and indignation.

When we pray for mercy and help in our time of need, we will find that our Lord's ear in heaven will be shut up from hearing us. Because of our iniquities and sins, our Lord *will not* hear us. Even so, the psalmist proclaimed in Psalm 66:18, *"If I regard iniquity in my heart, the Lord will not hear me."* Furthermore, our Lord proclaimed concerning His sinning people in Ezekiel 8:18, *"Therefore will I also deal in fury: mine eye shall not spare, neither will I have pity: and though they cry in mine ears with a loud voice, yet will I not hear them."*

In Proverbs 28:9 the judgment is given, *"He that turneth away his ear from hearing the law, even his prayer shall be abomination."* Even so, Zechariah 7:11-13 gives report concerning God's people who refused to hearken unto His Word, *"But they refused to hearken, and pulled away the shoulder, and stopped their ears, that they should not hear. Yea, they made their hearts as an adamant stone, lest they should hear the law, and the words which the LORD of hosts hath sent in his spirit by the former prophets:*

therefore came a great wrath from the LORD of hosts. Therefore it is come to pass, that as he cried, and they would not hear; so they cried, and I would not hear, saith the LORD of hosts." If we refuse to hear and obey the truth of God's Word, then He will refuse to hear and answer the cry of our prayers. God's ear in heaven will be shut up from us.

> **The Pursuits of Our Lives Will Become Fruitless**

The second characteristic of our Lord's chastening hand will be that our pursuits in life will be made more and more fruitless. The second possible case of chastening against His people that our Lord presented in 2 Chronicles 7:13 was, "*Or if I command the locusts to devour the land.*" At that time the nation of Israel was an agricultural society. The crops of the land represented the investment of their efforts in planting season and the success of their efforts through the harvest. Their prosperity was directly joined with the success of the harvest. For the locusts to devour the crops of the land was for their efforts in planting to be completely wasted and fruitless. Even so, this is suggestive and illustrative of our Lord's causing the efforts and pursuits of our lives to become fruitless and wasted.

In Leviticus 26:18-20 the Lord warned His people Israel through His servant Moses, saying, "*And if ye will not yet for all this hearken unto me, then I will punish you seven times more for your sins. And I will break the pride of your power; and I will make your heaven as iron, and your earth as brass: and your strength shall be spent in vain: for your land shall not yield her increase, neither shall the trees of the land yield their fruits.*" This is the character of our Lord's chastening hand upon us. The strength of our daily efforts and pursuits will be spent in vain, for the Lord will break the success of our power through His heavy hand of chastening.

Again in Deuteronomy 28:38-44 the Lord warned His people, saying, "*Thou shalt carry much seed out into the field, and shalt gather but little in; for the locust shall consume it. Thou shalt plant vineyards, and dress them, but shalt neither drink of the wine, nor gather the grapes; for the worms shall eat them. Thou shalt have olive trees throughout all thy coasts, but thou shalt not anoint thyself with the oil; for thine olive shall cast his fruit. Thou shalt beget sons and daughters, but thou shalt not enjoy them; for they shall go into captivity. All thy trees and fruit of thy land shall the locust consume. The stranger that is within thee shall get up above thee very high; and thou shalt come down very low. He shall lend to thee, and thou shalt not lend to him: he shall be the head, and thou shalt be the tail."*

Even so, in Haggai 1:5-6 the Lord confronted His sinful and selfish people, saying, *"Now therefore thus saith the LORD of hosts; Consider your ways. Ye have sown much, and bring in little; ye eat, but ye have not enough; ye drink, but ye are not filled with drink; ye clothe you, but there is none warm; and he that earneth wages earneth wages to put it into a bag with holes."* In addition, the Lord confronted them in the opening portion of verse 9, saying, *"Ye looked for much, and, lo, it came to little; and when ye brought it home, I did blow upon it."* Yes, this is the character of our Lord's chastening hand upon us. He will cause our great efforts to come unto little profit. Then He will blow upon that little until He blows it all away.

➤ The Spirit of Our Hearts Will Become Troubled

The third characteristic of our Lord's chastening hand will be that the spirit of our hearts will become more and more troubled. The third possible case of chastening against His people that our Lord presented in 2 Chronicles 7:13 was, *"Or if I send pestilence among my people."* This was not simply the Lord's hand against the crops of their land. This was the Lord's hand against the health of their bodies. The Lord would bring a pestilence against the people themselves. Even so, this is suggestive and illustrative of our Lord's afflicting us in the inner man with a fearful, troubled, disheartened spirit.

In Leviticus 26:36 the Lord warned His people Israel through His servant Moses, saying, *"And upon them that are left alive of you I will send a faintness into their hearts in the lands of their enemies; and the sound of a shaken leaf shall chase them; and they shall flee, as fleeing from a sword; and they shall fall when none pursueth."*

This is the character of our Lord's chastening hand upon us. If we will not hear and obey His Word, but despise His statutes and standards, then He will send a spirit of faintness into our hearts. A spirit of fear and worry will fill our hearts even when there is nothing about which to fear.

Again in Deuteronomy 28:28-29 the Lord warned His people, saying, "*The LORD shall smite thee with madness, and blindness, and astonishment of heart: and thou shalt grope at noonday, as the blind gropeth in darkness, and thou shalt not prosper in thy ways: and thou shalt be only oppressed and spoiled evermore, and no man shall save thee.*" When we are walking in sinful iniquity against Him, our Lord will chasten us with madness of mind, blindness of understanding, and astonishment of heart. We will grope through life from day to day, but will not find any help for the troubling of our hearts within us.

Yet again in Deuteronomy 28:65-67 the Lord warned His people, saying, "*And among these nations shalt thou find no ease, neither shall the sole of thy foot have rest: but the LORD shall give thee there a trembling heart, and failing of eyes, and sorrow of mind: and thy life shall hang in doubt before thee; and thou shalt fear day and night, and shalt have none assurance of thy life: in the morning thou shalt say, Would God it were even! and at even thou shalt say, Would God it were morning! for the fear of thine heart wherewith thou shalt fear, and for the sight of thine eyes which thou shalt see.*" Yes, this is the character of our Lord's chastening hand upon us – a trembling of heart, a failing of motivation, and a sorrow of mind. Day after day we shall pine away in the consuming hopelessness of depression and despair. "*There is no peace, saith my God, to the wicked.*" (Isaiah 57:21)

Yet there is a place of hope, if we will come to it. In 2 Chronicles 7:14 our Lord proclaimed, "*If my people, which are called by my name, shall humble themselves, and pray, and seek my face, and turn from their wicked ways; then will I hear from heaven, and will forgive their sin, and will heal their land.*" This place of hope is the ground of repentance. Certainly it is hard ground; yet it is also blessed ground.

Chapter Thirteen

If My People Shall Humble Themselves

As we have previously noted, our Lord's message in 2 Chronicles 7:12-14 was delivered as a direct response to Solomon's prayer concerning the temple in 2 Chronicles 6:14-42. Within this context the principle of verse 13 specifically concerns the chastening of our Lord against His sinning people. Then the opening portion of verse 14 presents the call of our Lord for His chastened people to repent of their sinful ways. *"If my people, which are called by my name, shall humble themselves, and pray, and seek my face, and turn from their wicked ways."* Herein we find four required ingredients to the ground of repentance and spiritual revival.

The Requirement of Humbling Ourselves

Now, the four conditions of 2 Chronicles 7:14 are not to be viewed as a series of four steps, but as a set of four ingredients. Genuine, Biblical repentance requires that we join all four ingredients together. Of these four ingredients, a specific reference is made to each of the latter three in Solomon's prayer. However, our Lord presents the ingredient of humbling ourselves at the beginning of the list because it is the foundational attitude upon which the other ingredients are founded. Without a true humbling of our hearts, we will not pray to the Lord in dependence, seek after the Lord in submission, or turn from our wicked ways in obedience.

A true humbling of our hearts before the Lord is the foundational requirement for spiritual revival. Yet what does it mean? When we go away backward from our Lord into sin, whether in attitude, word, or conduct, we willfully walk in the pride of selfishness and stubbornness. We focus our hearts upon the desires, pleasures, and interests of self. We forsake the will, ways, and Word of our Lord. We follow stubbornly more and more after that which displeases our Lord. We firmly stiffen our necks and harden our hearts against the chastening hand of our Lord.

Therefore, the foundational requirement for spiritual revival is the humbling of our selfish, stubborn hearts. We must come to the humble conviction that we are *not* right with our Lord and are *not* following after Him, but are in rebellion *against* our Lord and have *indeed* forsaken Him. We must come to humble contrition and brokenness of heart over our offense against our Lord and over our dishonor of our Lord. We must come to the humble confession that *"we have sinned,"* and *"have done amiss,"* and *"have committed iniquity, and have done wickedly,"* even in disobeying and departing from our Lord's precepts and principles. (2 Chronicles 6:37; Daniel 9:5)

We must humble ourselves as did Rehoboam and the princes of Israel in 2 Chronicles 12:5-8. *"Then came Shemaiah the prophet to Rehoboam, and to the princes of Judah, that were gathered together to Jerusalem because of Shishak, and said unto them, Thus saith the LORD, Ye have forsaken me, and therefore have I also left you in the hand of Shishak. Whereupon the princes of Israel and the king humbled themselves; and they said, The LORD is righteous. And when the LORD saw that they humbled themselves, the word of the LORD came to Shemaiah, saying, They have humbled themselves; therefore I will not destroy them, but I will grant them some deliverance; and my wrath shall not be poured out upon Jerusalem by the hand of Shishak. Nevertheless they shall be his servants; that they may know my service, and the service of the kingdoms of the countries."*

We must humble ourselves before the Lord our God as did Manasseh in 2 Chronicles 33:11-13. *"Wherefore the LORD brought upon them the captains of the host of the king of Assyria, which took*

Manasseh among the thorns, and bound him with fetters, and carried him to Babylon. And when he was in affliction, he besought the LORD his God, and humbled himself greatly before the God of his fathers, and prayed unto him: and he was intreated of him, and heard his supplication, and brought him again to Jerusalem into his kingdom. Then Manasseh knew that the LORD he was God."

We must humble ourselves as did the prodigal in Luke 15:17-18. *"And when he came to himself, he said, How many hired servants of my father's have bread enough and to spare, and I perish with hunger! I will arise and go to my father, and will say unto him, Father, I have sinned against heaven, and before thee, and am no more worthy to be called thy son: make me as one of thy hired servants."*

The Requirement of Praying to the Lord

The second ingredient to the ground of repentance and spiritual revival that our Lord presented in 2 Chronicles 7:14 is that of praying unto Him. In Solomon's prayer of dedication, a specific reference is made numerous times to this ingredient of prayer in repentance. We find this in 2 Chronicles 6:21, 24, 26, 29, 37-38. In every one of these cases, the need for forgiveness of sin is directly presented.

So then, the first request about which we must lift up our prayer unto the Lord is *for forgiveness and cleansing of sin.* Having humbled ourselves in conviction about our sin, contrition over our sin, and confession of our sin, we are then on the ground to ask our Lord for forgiveness from our sin's offense and for cleansing from our sin's filthiness. This was the prayer that Daniel lifted up in the opening portion of Daniel 9:19, saying, *"O Lord, hear; O Lord, forgive; O Lord, hearken and do."* This was the prayer that David lifted up in Psalm 51:1-2, saying, *"Have mercy upon me, O God, according to thy lovingkindness: according unto the multitude of thy tender mercies blot out my transgressions. Wash me throughly from mine iniquity, and cleanse me from my sin."*

Even so, Solomon prayed in the closing portion of 2 Chronicles 6:21, "*Hear thou from thy dwelling place, even from heaven; and when thou hearest, forgive.*" Again he prayed in the opening portion of verse 25, "*Then hear thou from the heavens, and forgive the sin of thy people Israel.*" Yet again he prayed in the opening portion of verse 27, "*Then hear thou from heaven, and forgive the sin of thy servants, and of thy people Israel, when thou hast taught them the good way, wherein they should walk.*" And yet again he prayed in the opening portion of verse 30, "*Then hear thou from heaven thy dwelling place, and forgive.*" Finally, he prayed in verse 39, "*Then hear thou from the heavens, even from thy dwelling place, their prayer and their supplications, and maintain their cause, and forgive thy people which have sinned against thee.*"

The second request about which we must lift up our prayer unto the Lord is *for deliverance from chastening and corruption.* Because of our sin, our Lord's righteous anger is kindled against us; our Lord's chastening hand is heavy toward us; and our own sin is bringing corruption upon us. Yet when we humble ourselves in conviction, contrition, and confession, we are then on the ground to ask our Lord that He turn away His righteous anger and remove His chastening hand from us. Then also we are on the ground to ask that He deliver us by His abundant grace and everlasting mercy from the corruption and destruction of our own sin in our lives. Yea, then we are on the ground to ask that He sow His grace and mercy where we have sown our sin and iniquity.

This was the prayer that Daniel lifted up in opening portion of Daniel 9:16, saying, "*O Lord, according to all thy righteousness, I beseech thee, let thine anger and thy fury be turned away from thy city Jerusalem, thy holy mountain.*" Again this was the prayer that Daniel lifted up in the opening portion of Daniel 9:18, saying, "*O my God, incline thine ear, and hear; open thine eyes, and behold our desolations, and the city which is called by thy name.*" This also was the prayer that David lifted up in Psalm 51:8, saying, "*Make me to hear joy and gladness; that the bones which thou hast broken may rejoice.*" This was the prayer that the psalmist lifted up in Psalm 85:4, saying, "*Turn us, O God of our salvation, and cause thine anger toward us to cease.*"

The third request about which we must lift up our prayer unto the Lord is *for restoration unto fellowship and favor*. When we humble ourselves in conviction, contrition, and confession, we are then on the ground to ask our Lord that He restore us unto daily, personal fellowship with Him. Then we are on the ground to ask that He replace the heaviness of His chastening in our lives with the blessedness of His fellowship. Then we are on the ground to ask that His face might no longer smite against us with anger, but that He now cause His face to shine upon us with favor.

This was the prayer that David lifted up in Psalm 51:11-12, saying, ***"Cast me not away from thy presence; and take not thy holy spirit from me. Restore unto me the joy of thy salvation; and uphold me with thy free spirit."*** This was the prayer that Daniel lifted up in Daniel 9:17, saying, ***"Now therefore, O our God, hear the prayer of thy servant, and his supplications, and cause thy face to shine upon thy sanctuary that is desolate, for the Lord's sake."*** This was the prayer that Asaph lifted up in Psalm 80:19, saying, ***"Turn us again, O LORD God of hosts, cause thy face to shine; and we shall be saved."*** This was the prayer that the psalmist lifted up in Psalm 85:6-7, saying, ***"Wilt thou not revive us again: that thy people may rejoice in thee? Shew us thy mercy, O LORD, and grant us thy salvation."***

The fourth request about which we must lift up our prayer unto the Lord is *for transformation of our hearts and lives*. It is not enough that we are forgiven and cleansed of our sins, that we are delivered from chastening and corruption, and that we are restored to fellowship and favor. If we truly humble ourselves in repentance of our sin, in conviction, contrition, and confession, then we will want to be spiritually transformed in our character so that we do not return unto our sin. This was the prayer that David lifted up in Psalm 51:10, saying, ***"Create in me a clean heart, O God; and renew a right spirit within me."*** This was the prayer of Asaph in the opening portion of Psalm 80:19, saying, ***"Turn us again, O LORD God of hosts."*** This was the prayer of the psalmist in the opening portion of Psalm 85:4, saying, ***"Turn us, O God of our salvation."***

The Requirement of Seeking after the Lord

The third ingredient to the ground of repentance and spiritual revival that our Lord presents in 2 Chronicles 7:14 is that of seeking His face. What then does this mean? Often we speak of seeking our Lord's face through prayer. Yet the matter of prayer was handled in the previous ingredient. Thus, in this context, seeking our Lord's face must refer to something beyond praying unto Him. In this context, seeking our Lord's face refers to walking with Him in fellowship and following after Him through obedience.

To seek the face of the Lord is to pursue *a walk of fellowship* with the Lord. It is to seek the Lord Himself. Psalm 105:4 gives the instruction, "***Seek the LORD, and his strength: seek his face evermore.***" We must seek an intimate, daily, moment-by-moment walk with the Lord our God. We must join with David in the commitment and desire of Psalm 63:1-2, saying, "***O God, thou art my God; early will I seek thee: my soul thirsteth for thee, my flesh longeth for thee in a dry and thirsty land, where no water is; to see thy power and thy glory, so as I have seen thee in the sanctuary.***" We must humbly return unto our Lord from our sinful ways and must earnestly enquire after a daily walk with Him. (Psalm 78:34)

To seek the face of the Lord is to pursue *a walk of obedience* to the Lord. Walking in fellowship with our Lord requires that we walk in obedience to our Lord. As Solomon indicated in his prayer of dedication for the temple, we must return unto the Lord from our sinful ways and must confess His holy name. (2 Chronicles 6:24) We must humbly confess Him as our Lord and Master and humbly submit ourselves to His will and ways. We must *return unto* Him with all our heart and with all our soul and must *seek after* Him with all our heart and with all our soul. (2 Chronicles 7:38; Deuteronomy 4:29) We must return unto the Lord our God and must "***be obedient unto His voice.***" (Deuteronomy 4:30) We must humbly submit ourselves to be taught "***the good way***," wherein we "***should walk.***" (2 Chronicles 6:27) We must humbly fear the Lord, to walk in His ways. (2 Chronicles 6:31)

The Requirement of Forsaking Wickedness

The fourth and final ingredient to the ground of repentance and spiritual revival that our Lord presents in 2 Chronicles 7:14 is that of turning from our wicked ways. Considering the placement of this ingredient as the last in the order, we should understand that this is more than a repentant confession of our sinful ways. The repentant confession of our sins and the humble request for forgiveness are encompassed under the previous ingredient of praying unto the Lord. Furthermore, in the order of the four ingredients, the ingredient of returning unto our Lord and following after Him precedes this ingredient of turning from our wicked ways. Yet the repentant confession of our sins is a Biblical prerequisite to return unto the fellowship of the Lord.

So then, this ingredient of turning from our wicked ways should be understood as a committed purpose and effort, through our Lord's enabling grace, to *forsake* a continuing practice in our sinful ways. Proverbs 28:13 includes the need for *both* confessing *and* forsaking our sins, saying, **"He that covereth his sins shall not prosper: but whoso confesseth and forsaketh them shall have mercy."** To enter into the fullness of spiritual revival, we must **"do works meet for repentance."** (Acts 26:20) Through our Lord's enabling grace, we must pursue after the actual correction and change of our character and conduct.

We must cast away from us all our transgressions, whereby we have transgressed against our Lord. (Ezekiel 18:31) We must **"lay apart all filthiness and superfluity of naughtiness."** (James 1:21) We must thoroughly amend our ways and our doings. (Jeremiah 7:5) We must **"lay aside every weight, and the sin which doth so easily beset us."** (Hebrews 12:1) Through the power of the indwelling Holy Spirit, we must mortify (put to death) the selfish, corrupt desires of our sinful flesh. (Romans 8:13; Colossians 3:5)

We must **"cast off the works of darkness"** and **"put on the armour of light."** (Romans 13:12) We must put on the Lord Jesus Christ, and cease to make any **"provision for the flesh, to fulfil the lusts thereof."** (Romans 13:14) The avenues and places through which the sin is committed must be restricted. The materials with which the sin is committed must be destroyed. The relationships in which the sin is committed must be severed. The actions by which the sin is committed must be avoided. The thoughts and meditations from which the sin is committed must be silenced. We must cast down every sinful imagination, *"**and every high thing that exalteth itself against the knowledge of God;**"* and we must bring *"**into captivity every thought to the obedience of Christ.**"* (2 Corinthians 10:5)

We must replace these avenues, places, materials, relationships, actions, thoughts, and meditations with those that would be pleasing unto the Lord our God. We must put away the evil of our doings from before our Lord's eyes. We must *"**cease to do evil**"* and *"**learn to do well.**"* (Isaiah 1:16-17; Psalm 34:14) We must *"**hate the evil, and love the good.**"* (Amos 5:15; Romans 12:9) We must put off all the sinful attitudes, communications, and actions of our sinful flesh (Colossians 3:8-9; Ephesians 4:22; 1 Peter 2:1), and must put on the righteousness and true holiness of the Lord our God (Colossians 3:12-17; Ephesians 4:24).

Chapter Fourteen

Then Will I Hear from Heaven

As we have previously noted, 2 Chronicles 7:13 presents a series of three conditional statements concerning *the chastening of our Lord* against His sinning people. Then the opening portion of verse 14 presents a series of four conditions concerning *the call of our Lord* unto His chastened people to repent of their sinful ways. Finally, the closing portion of verse 14 presents a series of three promises concerning *the commitment of our Lord* unto His repentant people.

When our Lord's hand of chastening is upon His people, if they will humbly repent of their sinful ways and return unto Him in humble submission, He gives the promise, ***"Then will I hear from heaven, and will forgive their sin, and will heal their land."*** This is a certain promise from the Lord our God. If we meet the prerequisite of humbling ourselves in repentance, praying unto the Lord in dependence, seeking after the Lord in submission, and turning from our wicked ways in obedience, we may have full assurance of faith that our Lord will be faithful to fulfill His promise.

Our Lord's Promise of Grace

The first promise that our Lord delivers in 2 Chronicles 7:14 to His repentant people is that He will ***"hear from heaven."*** This promise was given in direct response to Solomon's prayer of dedication in 2 Chronicles 6. Concerning God's people Israel when they would repent of their sinfulness, Solomon prayed in the opening line of verse 25, *"Then hear thou from the heavens."* Again concerning God's repentant people, Solomon prayed in the opening line of verse 27, *"Then hear thou from heaven."* Yet again concerning them, Solomon prayed in the opening line of verse 30, *"Then hear thou from heaven thy dwelling place."* Finally, concerning God's repentant people, Solomon prayed in the opening portion of verse 39, *"Then hear thou from the heavens, even from thy dwelling place, their prayer and their supplications."*

While we are walking against our Lord in sinful iniquity and stubborn rebellion, His righteous anger is kindled against us; and He shuts His ears unto our prayers. In Psalm 66:18 David revealed the principle, *"If I regard iniquity in my heart, the Lord will not hear me."* In Isaiah 1:15 our Lord Himself declared unto His spiritually backslidden people, *"And when ye spread forth your hands, I will hide mine eyes from you: yea, when ye make many prayers, I will not hear: your hands are full of blood."* In Isaiah 59:1-2 the truth is proclaimed, *"Behold, the LORD'S hand is not shortened, that it cannot save; neither his ear heavy, that it cannot hear: but your iniquities have separated between you and your God, and your sins have hid his face from you, that he will not hear."*

In Zechariah 7:11-12 our Lord gave report concerning His stubbornly rebellious people, saying, *"But they refused to hearken, and pulled away the shoulder, and stopped their ears, that they should not hear. Yea, they made their hearts as an adamant stone, lest they should hear the law, and the words which the LORD of hosts hath sent in his spirit by the former prophets: therefore came a great wrath from the LORD of hosts."* Then in verse 13 the chastening of the Lord was expressed, *"Therefore it is come to pass, that as he cried, and they would not hear; so they cried, and I would not hear, saith the LORD of hosts."* Even so, Proverbs 28:9 proclaims, *"He that turneth away his ear from hearing the law, even his prayer shall be abomination."*

Therefore, our Lord's promise in 2 Chronicles 7:14 to *"hear from heaven"* is His promise of grace unto His repentant people. When we are walking in stubborn rebellion against Him, His anger will be kindled against us; and He will shut His ears unto our prayers. Yet when we will come to humble repentance before Him, He will open His ears unto our prayers again; and His grace will be poured out upon us. Then He will *"hear from heaven"* and will provide His mercy and grace to help in our time of need. (Hebrews 4:16)

This is the very process that occurred in the case of King Manasseh. In 2 Chronicles 33:9-11 we read concerning Manasseh's sinful rebellion against the Lord and concerning the Lord's chastening hand against Manasseh. *"So Manasseh made Judah and the inhabitants of Jerusalem to err, and to do worse than the heathen, whom the LORD had destroyed before the children of Israel. And the LORD spake to Manasseh, and to his people: but they would not hearken. Wherefore the LORD brought upon them the captains of the host of the king of Assyria, which took Manasseh among the thorns, and bound him with fetters, and carried him to Babylon."*

Yet in verses 12-13 the situation changes with Manasseh's humble repentance before the Lord and with the Lord's gracious response unto Manasseh. *"And when he was in affliction, he besought the LORD his God, and humbled himself greatly before the God of his fathers, and prayed unto him: and he was intreated of him, and heard his supplication, and brought him again to Jerusalem into his kingdom. Then Manasseh knew that the LORD he was God."*

In like manner, we observe the case of King Josiah. In 2 Chronicles 34:27-28 the Lord's gracious message was delivered unto the king, saying, *"Because thine heart was tender, and thou didst humble thyself before God, when thou heardest his words against this place, and against the inhabitants thereof, and humbledst thyself before me, and didst rend thy clothes, and weep before me; I have even heard thee also, saith the LORD. Behold, I will gather thee to thy fathers, and thou shalt be gathered to thy grave in peace, neither shall thine eyes see all the evil that I will bring upon this place, and upon the inhabitants of the same. So they brought the king word again."*

"The LORD is merciful and gracious, slow to anger, and plenteous in mercy." (Psalm 103:8) *"He will not always chide"* with us over our sins. (Psalm 103:9) He will not retain His anger against us forever. He will not deal *"after our sins; nor rewarded us according to our iniquities."* (Psalm 103:10) He will not cause us to suffer under the full penalty that we justly deserve for our sins and iniquities. *"For as the heaven is high above the earth, so great is his mercy toward them that fear him* [that is – toward them that will humbly repent of their sins in godly fear before Him]." (Psalm 103:11)

Our Lord's Promise of Forgiveness

The second promise that our Lord delivers in 2 Chronicles 7:14 to His repentant people is that He will *"forgive their sins."* This promise also was given in direct response to Solomon's prayer of dedication in 2 Chronicles 6. Solomon prayed in the closing portion of verse 21, *"Hear thou from thy dwelling place, even from heaven; and when thou hearest, forgive."* Again Solomon prayed in the opening portion of verse 25, *"Then hear thou from the heavens, and forgive the sin of thy people Israel."* Yet again Solomon prayed in the opening portion of verse 27, *"Then hear thou from heaven, and forgive the sin of thy servants, and of thy people Israel, when thou hast taught them the good way, wherein they should walk."* And yet again Solomon prayed in the opening portion of verse 30, *"Then hear thou from heaven thy dwelling place, and forgive."* Finally, Solomon prayed in verse 39, *"Then hear thou from the heavens, even from thy dwelling place, their prayer and their supplications, and maintain their cause, and forgive thy people which have sinned against thee."*

The promise of our Lord is absolutely certain – *"If we confess our sins, he is faithful and just to forgive us our sins, and to cleanse us from all unrighteousness."* (1 John 1:9) He is eternally faithful and infinitely righteous to keep His promise. If we will humble ourselves in repentance, pray unto Him in dependence, seek after Him in submission, and turn from our wicked ways in obedience, He *will* "forgive us our sins." *"As far as the east is from the west,"* so far in His forgiveness will He remove *"our transgressions from us."* (Psalm 103:12) *"Like as a father pitieth his children, so the*

LORD pitieth them that fear him [that is – them that will humbly repent of their sins in godly fear before Him]." (Psalm 103:13)

Even so, in Isaiah 43:25 our Lord places great emphasis upon His promise of forgiveness, saying, *"I, even I, am he that blotteth out thy transgressions for mine own sake, and will not remember thy sins."* Thus with the motivation of this promise before us, our Lord gives His instruction in verses 26, *"Put me in remembrance: let us plead together: declare thou, that thou mayest be justified."* If we will remember our Lord and repent of our transgressions, our Lord will blot out in forgiveness the record of our transgressions and will not remember against us the guilt of our transgressions.

In like manner, Isaiah 55:6-7 gives the instruction for repentance and the promise of forgiveness, saying, *"Seek ye the LORD while he may be found, call ye upon him while he is near: let the wicked forsake his way, and the unrighteous man his thoughts: and let him return unto the LORD, and he will have mercy upon him; and to our God, for he will abundantly pardon."* Yes, if we will humbly repent of our sinful thoughts and ways, our Lord *will* mercifully and abundantly pardon our sins. Who is a God like unto the Lord our God, *"that pardoneth iniquity, and passeth by the transgression of the remnant of his heritage,"* that *"retaineth not his anger for ever, because he delighteth in mercy"*? (Micah 7:18) *"He will turn again, he will have compassion upon us; he will subdue our iniquities; and thou wilt cast all their sins into the depths of the sea."* (Micah 7:19)

Let us then join with the assurance and hope of the psalmist from Psalm 130:3-5, saying, *"If thou, LORD, shouldest mark iniquities, O Lord, who shall stand? But there is forgiveness with thee, that thou mayest be feared. I wait for the LORD, my soul doth wait, and in his word do I hope."* Yea, let us join with the prayer and assurance of David from Psalm 86:3-7, saying, *"Be merciful unto me, O Lord: for I cry unto thee daily. Rejoice the soul of thy servant: for unto thee, O Lord, do I lift up my soul. For thou, Lord, art good, and ready to forgive; and plenteous in mercy unto all them that call upon thee. Give ear, O LORD, unto my prayer; and attend to the voice of my supplications. In the day of my trouble I will call upon thee: for thou wilt answer me."*

Our Lord's Promise of Restoration

The third promise that our Lord delivers in 2 Chronicles 7:14 to His repentant people is that He will *"**heal their land.**"* Now, many have stumbled over the application of this promise unto the New Testament believer today. Some have misapplied the principle of this promise, applying it to our country as a national body, as if our nation is the chosen nation of God. Therein they have developed an expectation that is Biblically unwarranted. Others have misunderstood the principle of this promise, arguing that the "land promises" of the Old Testament are to be applied strictly unto God's chosen nation Israel. Therein they have denied any application of this principle unto the New Testament believer.

In truth, it must be understood that the "land promises" of the Old Testament were *not* specifically made to New Testament believers. Indeed, these promises were made to the nation of Israel as God's chosen *nation*. Our Lord has *not* promised *any* specific quantity or quality of land for this life to New Testament believers, either individually or corporately. In the time of the Old Testament, our Lord promised the blessings of an abundant *physical land* to His chosen nation Israel. In this time of the New Testament, our Lord has promised the blessings of an abundant *spiritual life* to His spiritually regenerate children. Even so, our Lord Jesus Christ declared in the closing portion of John 10:10, ***"I am come that they might have life, and that they might have it more abundantly."***

Yet this does not mean that the principle of our Lord's promise in 2 Chronicles 7:14 to *"**heal their land**"* has no application whatsoever unto us today. ***"For whatsoever things were written aforetime were written for our learning, that we through patience and comfort of the scriptures might have hope."*** (Romans 15:4) In this regard, it is important for us to remember the context of this promise. Yea, it is important for us to remember that 2 Chronicles 7:13-14 is all one lengthy sentence.

At the beginning of this sentence, our Lord presented three possible cases by which He Himself might bring His own hand against His people. As we have previously learned, these three cases represent our Lord's hand of chastening against His people because of their walk in sin against Him. In verse 13 our Lord stated, ***"If I shut up heaven that there be no rain, or if I command the locusts to devour the land, or if I send pestilence among my people."***

In the time of the Old Testament, the Lord chastened His chosen nation Israel by removing from them the blessings of the abundant land. Yet if His people would humble themselves in repentance, pray unto Him in dependence, seek after Him in submission, and turn from their wicked ways in obedience, the Lord promised to ***"heal their land."*** If His people would come to humble repentance before Him, the Lord would restore them unto the blessings of their abundant land.

The principle of this promise is that our Lord would remove His hand of chastening from His repentant people, and that He would restore His repentant people unto the place of His blessing. The *principle* of our Lord's promise is the removal of chastening from those who humbly repent and the restoration of blessing unto them. Certainly this principle has application today unto us who are God's spiritually regenerate children.

Our Lord does indeed chasten us when we walk in sin against Him. ***"For whom the Lord loveth he chasteneth, and scourgeth every son whom he receiveth."*** (Hebrews 12:6) Just as He chastened His chosen nation Israel by removing from them the blessings of their *abundant physical land*, even so He chastens us who are His spiritually regenerate children by removing from us the blessings of our *abundant spiritual life*.

Yet if we will come to humble repentance before Him, our Lord will remove His hand of chastening and restore His hand of blessing. Just as He promised to restore His chosen nation Israel unto the blessings of their abundant physical land if they came to humble repentance of their sinful ways, even so He will restore us who are His spiritually regenerate children unto the blessings of our abundant spiritual life if we come to humble repentance of our sinful ways.

If we humbly repent of our sinful ways, we can have full assurance of faith that our Lord will restore us unto all the fullness of His blessed fellowship. We should not expect Him to miraculously convert and transform our nation as a nation, nor should we expect Him to miraculously fix all of the social, political, and economical problems in our nation. Such an expectation would be a misapplication of our Lord's promise. On the other hand, if we humbly repent of our sinful ways, we can and should have full assurance of faith that our Lord will forgive us and cleanse us of our sins, that He will grant us His mercy and deliverance, that He will restore us to His blessed fellowship, that He will lead us in the way of righteousness, that He will fill us with His peace and joy, and that He will bring forth spiritual fruit through us unto the glory of His holy name. "***A broken and a contrite heart***" the Lord our God most certainly will "***not despise.***" (Psalm 51:17)

Psalm 51:1-3, 16-17

Have mercy upon me, O God,
according to thy lovingkindness:
according unto the multitude of thy tender mercies
blot out my transgressions.
Wash me throughly from mine iniquity,
and cleanse me from my sin.
For I acknowledge my transgressions:
and my sin is ever before me.

For thou desirest not sacrifice;
else would I give it:
thou delightest not in burnt offering.
The sacrifices of God are a broken spirit:
a broken and a contrite heart, O God,
thou wilt not despise.

Chapter Fifteen

The Sacrifices of God Are a Broken Spirit

In Psalm 51:16-17 is revealed a powerful truth concerning the nature of the Lord our God and concerning His desire for our daily living. Therein the man of God David proclaimed, *"For thou desirest not sacrifice; else would I give it: thou delightest not in burnt offering. The sacrifices of God are a broken spirit: a broken and a contrite heart, O God, thou wilt not despise."* By His very nature of goodness and graciousness, the Lord our God will not despise a broken and a contrite heart. This is the promise of His nature in His relationship with us. He will not refuse or reject such a broken and contrite heart in our lives. He will not trample such a heart under His feet with contempt. He will not despise such a heart, but will *delight* in it.

The Lord our God is not simply looking for our religious sacrifices. He does not simply desire for us to draw nigh unto Him with our mouths and to honor Him with our lips. (Isaiah 29:13) He does not simply delight in our good works and our righteous efforts outwardly. Our Lord is not simply looking for surface things. He is looking deeper. He is looking to the heart of the matter. He is looking upon the character of our *hearts*. Our Lord only desires and delights in the surface things when they flow out of a broken and a contrite heart. *"The sacrifices of God are a broken spirit."*

Our Lord first desires and delights in a broken and a contrite heart. So then, if we desire to enter into the revival promise of our Lord – if we desire for our Lord to restore us unto the blessings of His daily fellowship, if we desire for Him to be pleased with us in our daily walk, if we desire for Him to delight in us, and not to despise our sacrifices and service – then we *must* be of a broken and a contrite heart over our sinful ways and stubborn rebellion against Him.

David wrote this psalm under the inspiration of God the Holy Spirit in order to express the true brokenness and contriteness of his heart concerning his sin. As the divinely inspired introduction to this psalm announces, it was written – **"To the chief Musician, A Psalm of David, when Nathan the prophet came unto him, after he had gone in to Bathsheba."** David had sinned in committing adultery with Bathsheba, the wife of Uriah the Hittite. He had sinned further in scheming to cover up that sin of adultery. Finally, in his scheming He had sinned in murdering Uriah through the sword of the Ammonites. All of these things are revealed to us in 2 Samuel 11; and the closing statement of 2 Samuel 11:27 declares, **"But the thing that David had done displeased the LORD."**

The Rebellion of a Stubborn Heart

In Psalm 32:1-5 David presented a summary of his spiritual condition during this time in his life. In verses 1-2 he introduced the psalm with a proclamation concerning the blessing of a forgiven life, saying, **"Blessed is he whose transgression is forgiven, whose sin is covered. Blessed is the man unto whom the LORD imputeth not iniquity, and in whose spirit there is no guile."** However, in verses 3-5 he revealed the process by which an individual is moved to that blessed condition of a forgiven life.

This process begins with the rebellion of a stubborn heart. This is revealed through the opening four words of verse 3, wherein David gave the report, **"When I kept silence."** At this point in the process, David had refused to acknowledge and confess his sin. At this point he had refused to repent of his sin against the Lord. At this point he had refused to seek forgiveness and cleansing from the Lord. Rather, he had sought first to ignore his sinful condition and then to cover up his sinful conduct.

Certainly David knew that he had sinned against the Lord, that he had committed iniquity, that he done wickedly. Yet he would not humble himself in broken-hearted repentance for approximately a year's time (and possibly even some time more). After his sin of adultery with Bathsheba, he simply sent her home and expected to move on with his life as if nothing was amiss. He had had his one night affair. He had enjoyed the pleasures of sin for that moment. He expected simply to put his sin behind him and to proceed on his merry way.

Yet the Lord confronted David with his sin by causing Bathsheba to become pregnant while her husband was away in battle. This was the Lord's rebuke. Yet David did not respond with brokenness and repentance. Rather, he responded with stubbornness and rebellion. He did not confess his sin. Rather, he hardened his heart and pursued various schemes in order to cover up his sin.

Finally, in stubborn rebellion against the Lord, David set up Uriah, Bathsheba's husband, to be killed in battle. Then he married the widowed Bathsheba, publicly acting as if this was an act of mercy and comfort. In truth, this was just a part of David's rebellious scheme to cover up Bathsheba's pregnancy with his own child. Then throughout the remainder of Bathsheba's pregnancy and the birth of the child, David continued in rebellious satisfaction that his scheming had been successful, that the matter was settled, and that all was again well.

The Suffering of a Chastened Life

Yet all was not well, for 2 Samuel does not close with the success of David's rebellious scheming. Rather, it ends with a statement of the Lord's hot displeasure – "***But the thing that David had done displeased the LORD.***" Regardless of what David thought about the matter, his rebellious scheming was not successful. "***He that covereth his sins shall not prosper.***" (Proverbs 28:13) Rather, he that hardens his heart in stubborn rebellion shall fall under the Lord's heavy hand of chastening. He shall experience the suffering of a chastened life.

This is the work of our Lord by which He seeks to move an individual from the rebellion of a stubborn heart unto the blessing of a forgiven life. Even so, in Psalm 32:3-4 David continued his report, saying, *"When I kept silence, my bones waxed old through my roaring all the day long. For day and night thy hand was heavy upon me: my moisture is turned into the drought of summer. Selah."* Continually, both day and night, the Lord's hand of chastening was heavy upon David because he stubbornly and rebelliously refused to confess his sins in repentance. All day long the Lord's heavy hand of chastening poured out suffering upon David's heart and life.

Under the Lord's heavy hand of chastening, David suffered the removal of his strength. He indicated that his very bones waxed old. Through this poetic picture, he was revealing, not simply that the strength of his physical body was lost, but even more so that the strength of his inner man was lost. In Psalm 27:1 David gave the testimony, saying, *"The LORD is my light and my salvation; whom shall I fear? The LORD is the strength of my life; of whom shall I be afraid?"* At such a time when the Lord was the strength of his life, David's heart was filled with strength and courage. Yet under the Lord's heavy hand of chastening, the strength of David's heart was not renewed, but was removed. At that time his courage was lost, and fear took hold upon him. At that time his inner man "waxed old" and was made weak. At that time his heart was filled with discouragement and depression.

Under the Lord's heavy hand of chastening, David also suffered the fullness of deep sorrow. In fact, he indicated that his bones, the strength of his inner man, "waxed old" and were made weak specifically through his roaring with grief and sorrow "all the day long." In this context, the word "roaring" signifies the guttural cries and groanings of anguish that are wrung forth from an individual by the piercing pain of his deep sorrow and grief. The heaviness of the Lord's chastening hand pierced David's heart with continual grief and sorrow. "All the day long" his heart and soul were filled with trouble, and he could find no relief. At that time, although he may have experienced moments of happiness, he could find no lasting joy or peace in heart. At that time despair and bitterness became his common companions.

Finally, under the Lord's heavy hand of chastening, David suffered the loss of any satisfaction. He indicated that his moisture was turned into a summer drought. Through this poetic picture, he was revealing that his thirst for life (that is – for joy, happiness, peace, and hope) could not be satisfied. Even when his pursuits ended in outward success, they did not bring inward satisfaction. At that time the Lord's heavy hand of chastening was turning every pursuit into the dryness of a summer drought. At that time of chastening, no pursuit could strengthen David's heart, sustain his joy, or satisfy his soul. This is the suffering of a heart and life that is chastened under the heavy hand of our Lord.

The Confession of a Broken Heart

Yet there is a way of deliverance from the suffering of a chastened life. The Lord our God Himself has established this way of deliverance from His own chastening hand. In Proverbs 28:13 God's Word delivers God's promise, saying, "*He that covereth his sins shall not prosper: but whoso confesseth and forsaketh them shall have mercy.*" Again in 1 John 1:9 God's Word delivers God's promise, saying, "*If we confess our sins, he is faithful and just to forgive us our sins, and to cleanse us from all unrighteousness.*"

Understanding this principle and promise, David finally yielded under the Lord's chastening hand to the repentant confession of a broken and contrite heart. In Psalm 32:5 he declared, "*I acknowledged my sin unto thee, and mine iniquity have I not hid. I said, I will confess my transgressions unto the LORD; and thou forgavest the iniquity of my sin. Selah.*" Even so, in Psalm 51:16-17 he proclaimed, "*For thou desirest not sacrifice; else would I give it: thou delightest not in burnt offering. The sacrifices of God are a broken spirit: a broken and a contrite heart, O God, thou wilt not despise.*" David ceased to cover his sinful iniquity against the Lord. He ceased to continue in stubborn rebellion against the Lord. He turned unto the Lord in confession of his sin. He turned unto the Lord with contriteness of heart.

David had sought to cover his sin. He had continued in stubborn rebellion against the Lord concerning his sin for over a year's time. Throughout that time the Lord's hand of chastening was heavy upon him. Finally, the Lord sent the prophet Nathan to confront David with the message of God's Word. Through the reproof of God's Word, David's heart was pierced with conviction over his sinful iniquity. Under conviction David confessed his transgression against the Lord. In 2 Samuel 12:13 David proclaimed unto Nathan the prophet, *"I have sinned against the LORD."* In Psalm 51:3-4 he prayed unto the Lord, *"For I acknowledge my transgression: and my sin is ever before me. Against thee, thee only, have I sinned, and done this evil in thy sight: that thou mightest by justified when thou speakest, and be clear when thou judgest."* He repented of his sin with a broken and contrite heart.

The Blessing of a Forgiven Life

Even so, in the closing line of Psalm 32:5 David declared, *"And thou forgavest the iniquity of my sin. Selah."* No, the Lord our God will never despise a broken and a contrite heart over sin. Yes, if we will confess and forsake our sins with the broken and contrite heart of repentance, the Lord our God will certainly pour out His mercy upon us. Yea, then He will certainly be *"faithful and just to forgive us our sins, and to cleanse us from all unrighteousness."* (1 John 1:9) Then He will certainly have mercy upon us and *"will abundantly pardon."* (Isaiah 55:7)

Therefore, David was able to begin Psalm 32 in verses 1-2 with the proclamation, *"Blessed is he whose transgression is forgiven, whose sin is covered. Blessed is the man unto whom the LORD imputeth not iniquity, and in whose spirit there is no guile."* Oh, the blessing of a forgiven life! Oh, how blessed it is to experience our Lord's gracious and abundant forgiveness of our transgressions! Oh, how blessed it is to have the offense of our sin covered and the stain of our sin cleansed away, to have our sins blotted out and remembered no more!

Oh, how blessed it is to have the Lord our God no longer imputing the iniquity of our sins against us, to have His fiery wrath and chastening hand removed from us, and to have His blessed fellowship and merciful favor restored unto us! Oh, how blessed it is to have the spirit of our heart and mind renewed in righteousness and godliness through the power of the indwelling Holy Spirit!

Oh, how blessed it is to have our Lord's ear opened again unto our prayers! *"For this shall every one that is godly pray unto thee in a time when thou mayest be found: surely in the floods of great waters they shall not come nigh unto him."* (Psalm 32:6) Oh, how blessed it is to know that our Lord's mighty hand is no longer against us in chastening, but is now for us in protection and deliverance! *"Thou art my hiding place; thou shalt preserve me from trouble; thou shalt compass me about with songs of deliverance. Selah."* (Psalm 32:7)

Oh, how blessed it is to be restored unto the gentle, loving guidance of our Lord's fellowship, to be instructed and taught by Him in the way that we should go! *"I will instruct thee and teach thee in the way which thou shalt go: I will guide thee with mine eye."* (Psalm 32:8) Oh, how blessed it is to be surrounded again with the multitude of our Lord's tender mercies! *"Many sorrows shall be to the wicked: but he that trusteth in the LORD, mercy shall compass him about. Be glad in the LORD, and rejoice, ye righteous: and shout for joy, all ye that are upright in heart."* (Psalm 32:9-10)

Chapter Sixteen

A Broken and A Contrite Heart

As we have previously noted, the man of God David wrote Psalm 51 under the inspiration of God the Holy Spirit, in order to express the true brokenness and contriteness of his own heart concerning his sin. As the divinely inspired introduction to this psalm announces, it was written – ***"To the chief Musician, A Psalm of David, when Nathan the prophet came unto him, after he had gone in to Bathsheba."*** David had sinned in committing adultery with Bathsheba. He had then continued in stubborn rebellion, refusing to repent of his sin. He attempted to cover up his sin, rather than confess his sin. In all of this, the Lord was displeased with David and set His heavy hand of chastening upon David. Finally, the Lord sent the prophet Nathan to confront David with the message and rebuke of His Word.

At the rebuke of God's Word, David was brought to conviction and repentance of heart. In 2 Samuel 12:13 he cried out and said unto Nathan before the Lord with true brokenness of heart, ***"I have sinned against the LORD."*** Then immediately after these events, David wrote Psalm 51 under the inspiration of God the Holy Spirit. Yea, with this psalm he revealed how deeply and truly broken and contrite he was over his sin. Even so, this Psalm reveals the true nature of a truly broken and a truly contrite heart over sin.

In addition, David wrote this psalm under the inspiration of God the Holy Spirit in order to teach other sinners the true way of repentance and of returning unto the Lord their God. In Psalm 51:13, after praying for forgiveness, cleansing, transformation, and restoration, David committed himself unto the Lord, saying, *"**Then will I teach transgressors thy ways; and sinners shall be converted unto thee.**"* In fact, by this very psalm David has fulfilled that commitment down through the ages, even after his death. Even so, Psalm 51, as God's inspired Word, is God's own revelation concerning the ingredients and characteristics of a heart that is truly broken and contrite over its sin. As we study through this psalm, we shall learn those ingredients and characteristics.

Resting on Our Lord's Mercies

In Psalm 51:1 David prayed, *"**Have mercy upon me, O God, according to thy lovingkindness: according unto the multitude of thy tender mercies blot out my transgressions.**"* An individual with a truly broken and contrite heart recognizes the overwhelming greatness and wretchedness of his own sinful iniquity. He knows that he is in a miserable spiritual condition. He knows that spiritually he is in a horrible pit of miry clay. (Psalm 40:2) He knows that the mire of his own sins will continue to suck him deeper until it shall drown him in destruction. He knows that he has been taken captive by his own iniquities, and that he is held fast with the cords of his own sins. (Proverbs 5:22)

He knows that he has sown the wind, and that he must now reap the whirlwind. (Hosea 8:17) He knows that he has sown to his sinful flesh in yielding himself unto the pleasures of sin that only last for a season. He knows that now he must reap spiritual corruption. (Galatians 6:7-8) Now that the short season of sin's pleasure is over, he knows that spiritually he is in a dark, evil, bitter place. (Jeremiah 2:19) He knows that his miserable condition is his own fault. He knows that he has dug his own pit, yea his own grave, by his own sinful iniquity and stubborn rebellion.

Knowing all of this, the individual with a truly broken and contrite heart recognizes that the only ground for help and hope is the merciful nature of the Lord our God. He knows that all other ground is still miry clay. He knows that there is no help or hope within himself. He knows that he has sinned, that he has committed iniquity, that he has done wickedly, that he has rebelled against God. (Daniel

9:5) He knows that his heart is desperately wicked, and that he stands guilty before God. He desires forgiveness, cleansing, and restoration. Yet he knows that he is wholly unworthy of these things. He knows that his holy and righteous Lord God is a just Judge, and that God's justice demands his condemnation.

Oh yes, an individual with a truly broken and contrite heart knows the overwhelming greatness and wretchedness of his own sinful iniquity. He knows that he is completely unable to do anything to help himself out of this wretched condition. He knows that there is nothing in his own character in which to find hope. Yet he also knows that there is *infinitely much* in the nature of his merciful Lord God and Savior in which he may set his hope. Therefore, an individual with a truly broken and contrite heart will seek to be planted upon the only solid ground of spiritual help and hope. He will seek to be planted upon the only solid rock – the solid rock of our Lord's everlasting mercies. He will seek to put down his roots deeply in the loving kindness of the Lord his God. He knows no other hope!

An individual with a truly broken and contrite heart knows the greatness of his own sin. Thus he will look unto and set his trust upon the *multitude* of our Lord's tender mercies. He will cry out as David did in the closing portion of Psalm 51:1, **"According to the multitude of thy tender mercies blot out my transgressions."** Oh, what a blessed word is that word "multitude"! Only the infinite multitude of our Lord's tender mercies can possibly remove the wretchedness of our sinfulness and the greatness of our guilt. Here alone a truly broken and contrite heart rests – in the merciful nature and abundant mercies of the Lord our God.

A truly broken and contrite heart rests in the truth that our merciful Lord God is both *able* and *willing* to pardon and cleanse our sinful iniquity. It rests in the truth that our merciful Lord God is able to pardon and cleanse sinful iniquity, *no matter how great and terrible that sinful iniquity may be*. Furthermore, it rests in the truth that our merciful Lord God will pardon and cleanse sinful iniquity, *because He delights in showing mercy*. In Micah 7:18 God's Word exclaims, **"Who is a God like unto thee, that pardoneth iniquity, and passeth by the transgression of the remnant of his heritage? He retaineth** *not his anger for ever, because he delighteth in mercy. He will turn again, he will have compassion upon us; he will subdue our iniquities; and thou wilt cast all their sins into the depths of the sea."*

Oh, what a distinguishing characteristic this is in the nature of the Lord our God and Savior! Who is like unto Him? He alone is the *merciful* God. He is a God who *delights* in mercy. He is a God who is *"plenteous in mercy."* (Psalm 86:5) There is no mercy like unto the multitude of His tender mercies. Therefore, a truly broken and contrite heart will look wholly unto the merciful Lord God for His merciful forgiveness. Therefore, a truly broken and contrite heart will rest wholly in the undeserved mercy, tenderness, com-passion, and loving kindness of the Lord our God.

Seeking for Our Lord's Forgiveness

A truly broken and contrite heart that is wholly resting in the multitude of our Lord's tender mercies will then seek for forgiveness from the Lord according to His mercies. David opened Psalm 51:1 with the request, *"Have mercy upon me, O God."* Then at the end of the verse, David indicated the specific mercy for which he was praying at that time. *"According unto the multitude of thy tender mercies blot out my transgressions."* Herein David was asking for the forgiveness of his sins. Even so, in verse 9 he again expressed his request for the Lord's merciful forgiveness, praying, *"Hide thy face from my sins, and blot out all mine iniquities."*

In both verse 1 and verse 9, David employed the phrase, *"blot out."* This phrase means, "to wipe away." It might be illustrated in the picture of wiping words off a chalkboard. Through this phrase David was asking for a clean slate. He was not asking for the Lord simply to cross out the record of his sins and iniquities. Rather, he was asking for the Lord mercifully to blot out that record. He was asking for the very record of his sins and iniquities to be wiped away. Yea, David was asking that in the abundance of His mercy, the Lord might completely erase the very record of David's sinful iniquity from His record book, so that there would be no record that David had ever committed that sin. This is the prayer of the truly broken and contrite heart for forgiveness of sin.

Yet another picture of our Lord's merciful forgiveness is revealed in the opening half of verse 9 where David prayed, *"**Hide thy face from my sins.**"* David was here asking for the Lord no longer to look upon his sins. As long as the Lord our God looks upon our sins, He *will be* offended by them. The holy Lord God of heaven and earth *cannot* look upon sin, *and not be* offended. Furthermore, as long as we regard iniquity in our hearts with favor and refuse to repent thereof, the Lord our God *cannot* regard us without being offended. Finally, as long as the Lord our God is offended by our sinful iniquity, His anger *will be* kindled against us as sinners.

So then, an individual with a truly broken and contrite heart will ask for the Lord to hide His face from his sins and to look upon him for His goodness' sake. (Psalm 25:7) This is what it means for our Lord to cast our sins behind His back. (Isaiah 38:17) This is what it means for our Lord to cast our sins *"**into the depths of the sea.**"* (Micah 7:19) This is what it means for our Lord to remember our sin no more. (Jeremiah 31:34) In His abundant mercy, our merciful Lord will choose not to look upon our sins, be offended, and have His anger kindled against us. Rather, He will choose to blot out our sins, to wipe them away, to forgive us our sins. He will remove our sins from His sight so that He might look upon us with delight and open His hand of blessing upon us.

Seeking for Our Lord's Cleansing

In Psalm 51:2 David continued his prayer unto the Lord, saying, *"**Wash me throughly from mine iniquity, and cleanse me from my sin.**"* In verse 1 David asked for the Lord to forgive his sinful iniquities, to blot out his transgressions, to erase completely any record of his sins. Then in verse 2 David asked for something more. He not only desired for the Lord to wipe away *the guilt of his sinful iniquity*, but he also desired for the Lord to wash away *the filth of his sinful iniquity*.

Often when we sin against the Lord our God, we possess no real burden and brokenness over that sin, at least until we are caught. Then, after we have been caught in our sin, we are quick to make apologies. This is done so that *the guilt of our sin* might be removed, and so that we might avoid the punishment of our sin. Yet often we have no desire for *the filth of our sin* to be cleansed away. In such cases, we are burdened about *the guilt and punishment of our sin*; but we are not broken over *the filth and offense of our sin.*

This was the case with Pharaoh in Exodus 9:27-28. There we read, **"And Pharaoh sent, and called for Moses and Aaron, and said unto them, I have sinned this time: the LORD is righteous, and I and my people are wicked. Intreat the LORD (for it is enough) that there be no more mighty thunderings and hail; and I will let you go, and ye shall stay no longer."** Yes, Pharaoh acknowledged his sin and wickedness. Yet the focus of his acknowledgement was simply upon the removal of his punishment, "that there be no more mighty thunderings and hail." Indeed, Pharaoh was burdened about the guilt and punishment of his sin; but he was not broken over the filth and offense of his sin.

Moses recognized this truth concerning Pharaoh's heart. Thus we find his response in verses 29-30 – **"And Moses said unto him, As soon as I am gone out of the city, I will spread abroad my hands unto the LORD; and the thunder shall cease, neither shall there be any more hail; that thou mayest know how that the earth is the LORD'S. But as for thee and thy servants, I know that ye will not yet fear the LORD God."** Even so, verse 34 gives the report, **"And when Pharaoh saw that the rain and the hail and the thunders were ceased, he sinned yet more, and hardened his heart, he and his servants."**

Yet an individual with a truly broken and contrite heart will not only desire to be forgiven of his sin's guilt, but also to be cleansed from his sin's filth. In Psalm 51 David had come to view his sin as it truly was. He now viewed his sin as a dark, black stain *upon him.* He now viewed his sin as disgusting, hateful filth; and he no longer wanted any part with the disgusting, black filth of his sin. Therefore, he asked for the Lord to cleanse him from that filth. Yea, he asked for the Lord to wash him *thoroughly* from the filth of his sin.

David desired that the Lord would wash him inside and outside, from top to bottom, and all around. He asked for the Lord to wash him "throughly," all the way throughout, unto the very depths of his heart. He wanted to have no part with the filth of his sin any longer. He could feel the disgusting filth of his sin upon his heart, and he longed to be thoroughly washed from it. This is the attitude of a truly broken and contrite heart over sin. It understands the sin to be a disgusting filth, and it cannot wait to get under the shower of Christ's cleansing blood to be washed clean of sin's filth.

David also prayed and sought for *an active and vigorous* washing from the Lord. The word that he employed in the phrase "wash me" refers to the washing of a stain from clothing. In David's time such washing would be done by stomping or beating on the stained clothing while it was under water. This was the type of washing that David asked for the Lord to do upon him so that he might be thoroughly cleansed from his sin. He desired that the Lord would stomp his sin out of him. He desired that the Lord would so wash him that there would not be even a speck of his sin's filth and stain still upon him. Yes, an individual with a truly broken and contrite heart over sin will seek for the Lord *to cleanse him actively, vigorously, and thoroughly from his sin.*

Chapter Seventeen

For I Acknowledge My Transgressions

In Psalm 51 David expressed the true brokenness and contriteness of his own heart over his sin. In addition, David wrote this psalm under the inspiration of God the Holy Spirit in order to teach other sinners the true way of repentance and of returning unto the Lord their God. Even so, this Psalm reveals the true nature of a truly broken and contrite heart. As God's inspired Word, it is God's own revelation concerning the ingredients and characteristics of a heart that is truly broken and contrite over its sin.

Acknowledging Our Transgressions

Having asked in Psalm 51:1-2 for the Lord, in accord with the multitude of His tender mercies, to blot out and wash away his sinful iniquity, David continued in verse 3 with a confession of his sin. There he declared, *"**For I acknowledge my transgressions: and my sin is ever before me.**"* Even so, an individual with a truly broken and contrite heart over sin does not attempt to cover up that sin. Rather, such an individual will honestly and humbly acknowledge and confess his sin before the Lord our God.

As we have previously observed, at first David did *not* have a broken and contrite heart over his sin. For approximately one year's time, he did attempt to cover his sin. Yet as he wrote Psalm 51, David was no longer attempting to cover his sins. Rather, he was confessing and forsaking them. Even so, with a truly broken and contrite heart, we will not attempt to cover our sins. We will not seek for excuses to redefine our sins as acceptable, or at least tolerable in some sense. We will not make exceptions for ourselves, acknowledging that certain behavior may indeed be sin for others, but not for ourselves in our special case. No, with a truly broken and contrite heart, we will not make excuses for our sins or exceptions for ourselves. Rather, with a truly broken and contrite heart, we will acknowledge and face our sins directly and honestly.

Furthermore, with a truly broken and contrite heart, we will not shift the blame of our sins. We will not seek to convince ourselves that the blame for our own sins should actually be laid upon someone or something else. We will not blame our sins upon someone else's behavior or upon some circumstance outside ourselves. We will acknowledge that our sin, whatever it may be, is indeed *our own* sin against the Lord our God. We will not attempt to claim that our sin is actually someone else's fault. We will not attempt to claim that someone else caused our sin against God. We will honestly and humbly acknowledge that we ourselves caused our sin. No matter how another individual may have influenced us, we will acknowledge that our response of sin is indeed *our own* sin, and that *we ourselves* chose it.

Finally, with a truly broken and contrite in heart, we will view and acknowledge our sin to be as it truly is in our Lord's sight – utterly wicked and wretched. We will not attempt in any way to lighten the wickedness and wretchedness of our sin. In Psalm 51 David referred to his sin through the use of three different words. The first word that he employed is found in verse 1 and verse 3. It is the word "transgressions," and in both cases David used it in the plural. This word speaks of a willful, purposeful stepping out of the boundaries that the Lord our God has established. It is nothing less than *outright rebellion*. By using this word in the plural, David was acknowledging that he had, not just once, but over and over again rebelled against the Word and will of the Lord.

The second word that David employed is found in verse 2 and verse 9. It is the word "iniquity," and David used it in both the singular and the plural. This word speaks of perversion, of moral corruption, of a complete turning away from the righteous standard of God. It speaks of a morally, spiritually corrupt character. Indeed, this is true of all sin, whether it be a sin of action, word, or attitude. All sin is perversion.

The third word that David employed is found in verse 2, verse 3, and verse 9. It is the word "sin," and David also used it in both the singular and the plural. This word speaks of a complete missing of the mark that the Lord our God has set before us. It speaks of complete error and unrighteousness.

Such is the true picture of our sin; and with a truly broken and contrite heart, we will acknowledge our sin, no matter what it may be, as such. With a truly broken and contrite heart, we will face our sin directly. We will recognize the wretched nature of our sin. We will be deeply convicted of our wickedness. We will humbly cry out unto the Lord as David did – ***"For I acknowledge my transgressions: and my sin is ever before me."***

With a truly broken and contrite heart, we will humbly acknowledge unto the Lord our God that we have *rebelled* against Him. We will humbly acknowledge unto Him that we have *perverted* our hearts. We will humbly acknowledge unto Him that we have *completely missed* the mark of His righteous standard. We will humbly acknowledge unto Him that we have committed *utter wickedness* in His sight. We will humbly acknowledge that we *unquestionably* and *inexcusably* stand *unrighteous* before Him.

Recognizing Our Sin's Offensiveness

With just such deep conviction of unrighteousness and wickedness, David cried unto the Lord in the opening portion of verse 4, saying, ***"Against thee, thee only, have I sinned, and done this evil in thy sight."*** Indeed, as a disgusting filth, an unrighteous perversion, a rebellious wickedness, our sin greatly offends our all-holy Lord God. Certainly David had also sinned against Bathsheba and against Uriah her husband. Yet at this moment of confession, he was only concentrating upon his sinful iniquity and wicked offense against the Lord his God. He understood that all sin is first and foremost against the Lord. He understood that all sin is first and foremost *a direct attack* against the Lord and *a direct offense* unto the Lord. He understood that far above any other negative aspect of his sin on the lives of others, his sin was first and foremost an evil in the sight of the Lord his God.

This is the view of a truly broken and contrite heart over sin. With a truly broken and contrite heart, we will view our sin, whether in attitude, word, or action, as *absolute evil* against the Lord our God and Savior. We will view our sin as spiritual darkness and blackness. We will view our sin as a terrible abomination and a hateful thing. In the light of our Lord's pure holiness, we will view our sin as the most corrupt, perverse, wretched wickedness. With a truly broken and contrite heart, we will recognize the absolute offensiveness of our sin against our all-holy Lord God.

Accepting Our Lord's Judgment

In the closing portion of verse 4, David continued his declaration unto the Lord, saying, "***Against thee, thee only, have I sinned, and done this evil in thy sight: that thou mightest be justified when thou speakest, and be clear when thou judgest.***" This latter portion of the verse builds upon the beginning portion of the verse. Herein David was revealing the truth that because all sin is first and foremost against the Lord our God, He is righteous and just in judging all sin. He has every right to judge sin however He wills. Yet there is more to David's statement. He was not simply declaring a Biblical truth. He was also surrendering himself to that truth. David was acknowledging and accepting that the Lord's judgment of his own sin was a just and righteous judgment.

The Lord's judgment for this particular sin in David's life is recorded in 2 Samuel 12:10-12. There the prophet Nathan proclaimed unto David, "***Now therefore the sword shall never depart from thine house; because thou hast despised me, and hast taken the wife of Uriah the Hittite to be thy wife. Thus saith the LORD, Behold, I will raise up evil against thee out of thine own house, and I will take thy wives before thine eyes, and give them unto thy neighbour, and he shall lie with thy wives in the sight of this sun. For thou*** *didst it secretly: but I will do this thing before all Israel, and before the sun.*" Also in verse 14 the prophet of the Lord added, "*Howbeit, because by this deed thou hast given great occasion to the enemies of the LORD to blaspheme, the child also that is born unto thee shall surely die.*"

In Psalm 51:4, with a truly broken and contrite heart, David was expressing his acceptance of the Lord's judgment. He understood the truth of Biblical confession as revealed in Leviticus 26:40-41 – "*If they shall confess their iniquity, and the iniquity of their fathers, with their trespass which they trespassed against me, and that also they have walked contrary unto me; and that I also have walked contrary unto them, and have brought them into the land of their enemies; if then their uncircumcised hearts be humbled, and they then accept of the punishment of their iniquity . . . .*"

Certainly we find in 2 Samuel 12:15-23 that David prayed and fasted, if perchance the Lord would be gracious and allow the child to live. Yet even when the child died, David accepted the Lord's judgment and *worshipped Him*. Why did he do this? He did this because he knew that he *deserved* the Lord's judgment. In fact, he knew that he deserved far worse than the Lord had given him. He knew that the Lord had been gracious to him, and that the Lord had not dealt with him according to his sins.

Even so, with a truly broken and contrite heart over our sin, we ourselves will wholly accept the judgment of the Lord our God in our lives against our sin. Yes, as David did, we may pray that our Lord might be gracious in our time of need to relieve us from some of the consequences of our sin. Yea, in the multitude of His tender mercies, He might do just that. Yet with a truly broken and contrite heart, we will not argue with His righteous judgment even if He does not relieve us of those consequences. We will not complain against our Lord's judgment, nor will we be angered and embittered by it. We will know that our Lord's judgment is *right*. Yea, we will know that our Lord's judgment is *merciful*. We will know that we deserve far greater judgment than our Lord has given us. Thus we will be *thankful* for our Lord's merciful dealings with us, because He has not dealt with us according to our sin.

Admitting Our Sinful Character

Having acknowledged his transgressions, recognized his sin's offensiveness against the Lord, and accepted the righteousness of the Lord's judgment, David then acknowledged his sinful character in Psalm 51:5, saying, *"Behold, I was shapen in iniquity; and in sin did my mother conceive me."* Now, David was not here condemning his mother or indicating that she had conceived him in a sinful manner. He was not trying to shift the blame of his sin onto his mother. Rather, he was acknowledging that he himself possessed a nature that was bent toward sin, even from his very conception.

Even so, David was acknowledging more than that he had committed some wicked sins against the Lord. He was also admitting that those wicked sins flowed out of *a wicked, sinful heart*. He was admitting and acknowledging the wicked, ungodly character of his own heart. He was applying the truth of Jeremiah 17:9 to himself, admitting before God that his own heart was *"deceitful above all things, and desperately wicked."* David was admitting that he had *a heart problem*, and that he needed the Lord, not only to forgive the guilt of his sin and to cleanse the filth of his sin, but also to transform the character of his heart.

This is the nature of a truly broken and contrite heart over sin. A truly broken and contrite heart cries out with the apostle Paul from Romans 7:18, saying, *"For I know that in me (that is, in my flesh,) dwelleth no good thing."* Again a truly broken and contrite heart cries out with the apostle from Romans 7:24, saying, *"O wretched man that I am!"* Yet again a truly broken and contrite heart cries out with the prophet Isaiah from Isaiah 6:5, saying, *"Woe is me! For I am undone."* With a truly broken and contrite heart, we will face our sin directly and will admit the corrupt and carnal character *of our own hearts*. We will understand that our sins of attitude, word, and action reveal a problem *in our hearts*.

Recognizing Our Lord's Standard

In Psalm 51:5 David was brought to face the corruption and carnality of his own heart. It was an intense encounter with the truth, as the opening word "behold" reveals. Then in verse 6 David had a second intense encounter with a corresponding truth. Again the verse begins with the word "behold." Now he is brought to face the Lord's standard of a pure and holy heart. In verse 6 David proclaimed, "***Behold, thou desirest truth in the inward parts: and in the hidden part thou shalt make me to know wisdom.***"

The emphasis of this verse is clearly upon the inner man, upon the character of our hearts. Even so, in 1 Samuel 16:7 our Lord revealed the truth unto the prophet Samuel, saying, "***For the LORD seeth not as man seeth; for man looketh on the outward appearance, but the LORD looketh on the heart.***" The Lord our God is not pleased with the honor of our lips and the purity of our high moral standards, if our hearts are far from Him. He is not pleased when we are apparently clean on the outside of our lives, buffed, polished, and well groomed, if the character of our hearts is full of selfishness and sin, carnality and corruption.

The Lord our God is not looking for an external *form* of godliness. He is not looking for a *show* of godliness in our outward appearance. He is looking beyond the outward appearance. He is looking upon our hearts. He is examining our inner thoughts, our inner desires, and our inner motivations. The Lord our God desires that we walk "***in righteousness and true holiness.***" (Ephesians 4:23) In order for such righteousness and holiness to be *true*, it must be in our hearts. If it is only in our outward appearance, and not in our hearts, it is a *false* righteousness and holiness.

Even so, with a truly broken and contrite heart, we will recognize this truth and will wholly yield ourselves to it. We will not be satisfied when we outwardly appear righteous unto men. Rather, we will seek for our Lord to search us and to know *our hearts*, to try us and to know *our thoughts*. (Psalm 139:23) We will seek for our Lord to point out any and all of the wicked ways that are *within us*. (Psalm 139:24) Then we will humbly seek for our Lord to correct the character of our hearts and to lead us forth by His right way.

This is the nature of a truly broken and contrite heart over sin. In addition, this is the place where Psalm 51:6 not only confronts the character of our hearts, but also gives comfort and hope unto our hearts. In the opening half of the verse, David declared, "***Behold, thou desirest truth in the inward parts.***" That is the standard of the Lord our God. Yet in the closing half of the verse, David also declared with assurance and hope, "***And in the hidden part thou shalt make me to know wisdom.***" That is the provision and promise of the Lord our God. "***A broken and a contrite heart, O God, thou wilt not despise.***"

If we come unto the Lord our God with a truly broken and contrite heart, recognizing the corruption of our hearts in the light of our Lord's holy standard, He will begin His mighty work of transformation in us. At that very place, our Lord will begin His great and mighty work in us to transform the character of our hearts and to guide the direction of our lives in His righteousness and true holiness. Indeed, this is the place of hope, help, comfort, encouragement, and assurance. Indeed, this is the place of spiritual revival.

Chapter Eighteen

Create in Me a Clean Heart

Psalm 51 reveals the nature of a truly broken and contrite heart. As God's inspired Word, it is God's own revelation concerning the ingredients and characteristics of a heart that is truly broken and contrite over its sin. From the first six verses of this Psalm, we have already learned that a truly broken and contrite heart rests on our Lord's mercy, seeks our Lord's forgiveness and cleansing, acknowledges its transgressions, recognizes the offensiveness of its sins, accepts our Lord's judgment, admits its sinful character, and recognizes our Lord's standard of true holiness.

Finding Assurance and Hope in the Lord

In verse 7 David prayed unto the Lord, *"Purge me with hyssop, and I shall be clean: wash me, and I shall be whiter than snow."* Herein David presented two similar requests. In the opening half of the verse, He made the request, *"Purge me with hyssop."* In the closing half of the verse, he made the request, *"Wash me."*

Now, David had already expressed this request for spiritual cleansing in verse 2, praying, *"Wash me throughly from mine iniquity, and cleanse me from my sin."* Yet in verse 7 he added something more. In this verse he also expressed his assurance and hope in the Lord. In the opening half of the verse, he prayed unto the Lord for purging and then declared, *"And I shall be clean."* Again in the closing half of the verse, he prayed unto the Lord for washing and then declared, *"And I shall be whiter than snow."* Herein David's focus had settled upon the abundant grace and tender mercies of the Lord. Yea, herein his focus had settled with full assurance of faith upon the *promise and power* of our Lord's abundant grace and tender mercies to change his heart and life.

Yes, our Lord *will* show abundant grace and tender mercy toward the truly broken and contrite heart. Yes, our Lord *will* purge and wash away the filth and stain of sin from such a heart. In addition, when our Lord, in the infinite power of His abundant grace and tender mercies, purges and washes such a heart, He will do a thorough job. He will purge us and wash us even unto the very depths of our hearts. He will purge us and wash us until all is whiter even than newly fallen snow. According to the power and abundance of His grace and mercy, He *will* forgive our sins and *will* cleanse us from *all* our unrighteousness. **"If we confess our sins, he is faithful and just to forgive us our sins, and to cleanse us from all unrighteousness."** (1 John 1:9) Though our sins may be **"as scarlet, they shall be as white as snow;"** though they may be **"red like crimson, they shall be as wool."** (Isaiah 1:18)

This is the assurance and hope of a truly broken and contrite heart. The place of a truly broken and contrite heart is not a place of discouragement and despair. It is the best possible place for us to be. According to Isaiah 57:15, it is the place where the Lord our God will revive us again spiritually and will walk with us in fellowship. According to Psalm 51:17, it is the place where the Lord our God will be pleased with us and will bless us. A broken and a contrite heart is the very heart that the Lord our God *will not* despise. A broken and a contrite heart is the very heart upon which the Lord our God *will* pour out the abundance of His grace and the multitude of His tender mercies. A broken and a contrite heart is the very heart to which the Lord our God *will* speak comfortably. Yes, it may be hard ground. Yet it is also blessed ground.

Seeking for True Joy in the Lord

With full assurance in the Lord, David prayed in Psalm 51:8, saying, **"Make me to hear joy and gladness; that the bones which thou hast broken may rejoice."** Again in the opening half of verse 12, he prayed, **"Restore unto me the joy of thy salvation."**

Let us be honest with our own hearts. In our flesh we find pleasure and enjoyment in sin, at least initially. In fact, it is often through the carnal pleasures and enjoyments of sin that we are enticed to commit that sin. Even the Lord our God through His Holy Word recognizes that we may find pleasure and enjoyment in sin initially. In Hebrews 11:24-25 God's Word states concerning the man of God Moses, ***"By faith Moses, when he was come to years, refused to be called the son of Pharaoh's daughter; choosing rather to suffer affliction with the people of God, than to enjoy the pleasures of sin for a season."***

Yet Hebrews 11:25 also reveals the truth that the carnal pleasures and enjoyments of sin are only "for a season." The carnal pleasures and enjoyments of sin do not last and cannot give true joy. Even so, James 1:14 declares, ***"But every man is tempted, when he is drawn away of his own lust, and enticed*** [by the carnal pleasures and enjoyments of sin]." Yet verse 15 continues, ***"Then when lust hath conceived, it bringeth forth sin: and sin, when it is finished, bringeth forth death."***

When it is *finished*, sin does *not* bring forth pleasure, enjoyment, or fullness of joy. When it is *finished*, sin only brings forth destruction and death. Sin may be pleasurable for the moment, but *in the end* it is utterly destructive. Sin may be enjoyable for the moment, but it *cannot* fill our hearts with true, deep, lasting joy. Sin cannot fill our hearts with ***"joy unspeakable and full of glory."*** (1 Peter 1:8) There is only one place where we may find such true, deep, lasting, full, unspeakable, glorious joy. That place is not in sin, but in our Savior. Such a joy as this can *only* be found in our Lord.

A truly broken and contrite heart over sin knows and understands these things. In fact, with a truly broken and contrite heart, we will look past the temporary, carnal pleasures of sin, and will honestly face the destructive consequences of sin. We will see sin in its true light. We will see our sin in the light of our Lord God's holiness, and not in the light of sin's tempting enjoyments. We will see our sin, not as pleasurable and enjoyable, but as wretched and hateful. We will see our sin as that which brings misery and destruction. With a truly broken and contrite heart, we will see the wretchedness and destructiveness of our own sin and will turn away from the temporary pleasures and enjoyments that sin offers.

Furthermore, with a truly broken and contrite heart, we will be drawn again unto the Lord our God. We will desire to walk again with our Lord in the high and holy place of His blessed fellowship. We will long to be there, wherein is true joy, peace, and blessing. We will long to be there, wherein is everlasting satisfaction. We will look unto our Lord, seeking to hear His joy and gladness *ringing* within our hearts. Even so, David prayed in Psalm 51:8, *"**Make me to hear joy and gladness.**"* He prayed for the Lord Himself to fill him with the eternal joy and gladness that can be found *only* from and in the Lord.

Yet David's prayer in verse 8 was not just that he might experience the heights of spiritual joy in the Lord. It was also that he might be spiritually healed from the wounds of the Lord's chastening hand. Thus he continued his prayer, saying, *"**Make me to hear joy and gladness; that the bones which thou hast broken may rejoice.**"* Oh, how great is the crushing weight of our Lord's almighty hand when it continues heavy upon us in chastening! Yet when we repent of our sin with a truly broken and contrite heart, we may pray that the bones which were broken under our Lord's heavy hand might rejoice again through our Lord's healing hand.

This joy begins with the forgiveness of our sins through repentance with a truly broken and contrite heart. Even so, in verse 9 David repeated his request for forgiveness from verse 2, saying, *"**Hide thy face from my sins, and blot out all mine iniquities.**"* So many of us who are God's children lack joy because we will not confess our sins with a truly broken and contrite heart. The sins that we are stubbornly regarding in our hearts have destroyed our joy. Until we come to the place of brokenness over our sins, we will never find the place of joy in our Lord.

Seeking for Spiritual Transformation from the Lord

Having prayed for cleansing in verse 7, for joyfulness in verse 8, and for forgiveness in verse 9, David then prayed for complete transformation of heart and spirit in verse 10. He cried unto the Lord, saying, *"**Create in me a clean heart, O God; and renew a right spirit within me.**"* David was not satisfied with the forgiveness and cleansing of his sins. He desired something more. He desired something deeper. With a truly broken and contrite heart over his sin, he desired a completely renewed heart and spirit. He desired for the Lord to create within him a clean heart and a right spirit. He desired for a heart and spirit that would not *return* to sin.

Indeed, with a truly broken and contrite heart over our sins, we will understand our need for more than the forgiveness and cleansing of our sins. We will understand our need for the Lord our God to create in us a clean heart – a heart that is no longer filled with carnal desires, but with clean desires. We will understand our need for the Lord our God to renew in us a right spirit – a spirit that is no longer characterized by unrighteousness, but by the righteousness of the Lord our God Himself. We will understand our need for the Lord our God, by His almighty power and all-sufficient grace, to *transform* the character of our hearts and spirits.

Yea, with a truly broken and contrite heart, we will hunger and thirst after this transforming work of our Lord. We will fervently pray and earnestly plead for our Lord to create in us a clean heart and renew in us a right spirit. Yes, we will desire for the guilt and filth of our sin to be removed through forgiveness and cleansing. Yet we will also desire for future temptation to be resisted through a spiritually transformed character. Therefore, with a truly broken and contrite heart, we will desire and pray for our Lord to transform the character of our inner man. We will desire and pray for our Lord to transform the spirit of our minds and the motivation of our hearts.

Seeking for Restored Fellowship with the Lord

In verses 11-12 David revealed the primary interest of his broken and contrite heart. That primary interest was for a restored fellowship with the Lord his God. In verse 11 he presented that primary interest from the negative perspective, praying, "***Cast me not away from thy presence; and take not thy holy spirit from me.***" Then in verse 12 he presented that primary interest from the positive perspective, praying, "***Restore unto me the joy of thy salvation; and uphold me with thy free spirit.***" The reason that David sought for the forgiveness and cleansing of his sin was that he might be restored unto fellowship with the Lord. The means by which David sought for joyfulness of heart and transformation of character was through a restored fellowship with the Lord.

In the opening half of verse 11, David prayed, "***Cast me not away from thy presence.***" As we have previously learned, with a truly broken and contrite heart, we will understand that our sin is a great offense and evil in the sight of our all-holy Lord God. Furthermore, we will understand that our all-holy Lord God *cannot* and *will not* walk in fellowship with us while we are walking in the spiritual darkness of our sin. (1 John 1:5-7) Therefore, with a truly broken and contrite heart, we will recognize that our own sinful iniquities have separated between us and our Lord. (Isaiah 59:2) We will recognize that our own sin has broken our fellowship with the Lord and has created a barrier of division between us.

Yet with a truly broken and contrite heart, we will also earnestly desire to dwell with our Lord in the spiritual fellowship of His high and holy place. Yea, we will be fully convinced that there is no better place to be. Thus with a truly broken and contrite heart, we will fervently pray that our Lord might not cast us away from His presence (that is – from the favor of His blessed fellowship). We will fervently pray for our Lord to be gracious unto us according to the multitude of His tender mercies and to restore us unto a walk of close, intimate fellowship with Him.

Oh, how blessed is the answer of our Lord! Indeed, our Lord is a God of abundant grace who delights in mercy. "***A broken and a contrite heart, O God, thou wilt not despise.***" If we come unto Him with a truly broken and contrite heart, He *will not* turn a deaf ear unto us. He *will not* harden His heart against us. He *will not* turn His back upon us. Rather, He *will rejoice* in our repentance. He *will forgive*. He *will cleanse*. He *will restore*. He *will speak comfortably*. He *will revive us again*. He *will draw us close* in fellowship. He *will pour out* upon us the riches of His fellowship. He *will make our cups to run over* in His fellowship.

Again in the closing half of Psalm 51:11, David prayed, "***And take not thy holy spirit from me.***" With a truly broken and contrite heart, we will understand that our sin grieves and quenches the indwelling Holy Spirit of God. Certainly, the earnest and seal of the indwelling Holy Spirit, which we receive at the moment of our faith in Christ for salvation, will *never* be taken from us until the day of our final redemption and glorification. (Ephesians 1:13-14) Yet when we walk in sin, *the filling influence, daily guidance, and victorious power of the indwelling Holy Spirit* will be driven away by that sin. Thus with a truly broken and contrite heart, we will earnestly long and fervently pray for our Lord to fill us again with the holy influence, righteous direction, godly wisdom, and victorious power of His indwelling Holy Spirit. Even so, the blessed and gracious answer of our Lord will be, "Yes, my child, I will."

Yet again, in the opening half of Psalm 51:12, David prayed, "***Restore unto me the joy of thy salvation.***" Not only did David desire for the restored fellowship of the Lord's presence and for the filling influence of the Holy Spirit, but also he desired for the blessed and matchless joy of that fellowship. Already David had prayed for a restored joy in verse 8, saying, "***Make me to hear joy and gladness; that the bones which thou hast broken may rejoice.***" Yet here in verse 12 he was not simply asking for his heart to be filled with joy and gladness. Here David was asking specifically for the joy *of the Lord's salvation.*

In John 17:3 our Lord Jesus Christ defined eternal life and eternal salvation, saying, "***And this is life eternal, that they might know thee the only true God, and Jesus Christ, whom thou hast sent.***" So then, the joy of our salvation is the joy of knowing God our heavenly Father and Jesus Christ our Lord. It is the joy of walking *in fellowship with* God our heavenly Father and Jesus Christ our Lord. Even so, Psalm 16:11 reveals that in the fellowship of our Lord's presence "***is fulness of joy.***" Such is the joy for which a truly broken and contrite heart will earnestly desire and fervently pray – not just for fullness of joy in heart, but for the specific joy that comes through fellowship with our Lord.

Finally, in the closing half of Psalm 51:12, David prayed, *"**And uphold me with thy free spirit.**"* Here David was praying for the Lord graciously to set his feet upon a rock and establish his goings. He was praying for the Lord graciously to establish, strengthen, and settle him in the way of righteousness. He was praying for the Lord graciously to uphold him with the right hand of His righteousness and to keep his foot from slipping into further sin.

Even so, with a truly broken and contrite heart, we will fervently pray for the blessed peace and stability of our Lord's fellowship. We will not attempt to go forward in righteousness by our own ability. Rather, we will recognize that we can only go forward in righteousness through the upholding work of our Lord's almighty, everlasting arm. We will humbly recognize that we must continue abiding in Christ and allowing Him to abide in us. (John 15:4) We will humbly recognize that without Him we can do nothing. (John 15:5) With a truly broken and contrite heart, we will ever be praying for our Lord to *"**lead us not into temptation, but deliver us from evil.**"* (Matthew 6:13)

Chapter Nineteen

Then Will I Teach Transgressors

Throughout Psalm 51:1-12, with a truly broken and contrite heart, David prayed for the forgiveness and cleansing of his sin, for the spiritual transformation of his character, and for the restored joy and grace of the Lord's fellowship. Resting upon the multitude of the Lord's tender mercies, David had full assurance of faith that the Lord had answered and would continue to answer his prayer. Therefore, David proceeded to make a two-fold *commitment* unto the Lord. Even so, with a truly broken and contrite heart, we also will commit ourselves *to live unto the Lord our God*.

Pursuing after the Conversion of Other Sinners

In verse 13 David expressed his first commitment unto the Lord, saying, **"Then will I teach transgressors thy ways; and sinners shall be converted unto thee."** Having personally experienced the Lord's forgiving mercy, cleansing grace, transforming power, restored fellowship, abundant joy, spiritual guidance, and upholding love, David committed himself to pursue after the conversion of other sinners. He committed himself to pursue after other sinners that he might teach them the way of repentance and of return unto the Lord. He committed himself to pursue after other sinners that they might be converted from their sinful ways unto the righteous ways of the Lord.

Indeed, with a truly broken and contrite heart, we will not only desire to be free from the bondage and corruption of our own sins, but also to see other sinners free from the bondage and corruption of their sins. With a truly broken and contrite heart, we will not be self-directed in heart. Rather, we will first be God-directed, and then others-directed. We will be deeply committed to the glory of the Lord our God and to the conversion of sinners unto the Lord our God.

With a truly broken and contrite heart, we will earnestly and fervently seek after souls who are spiritually and eternally lost in their sins. We will earnestly and fervently seek after them in order that we may teach them the gospel truth of eternal salvation through faith in God the Son, the Lord Jesus Christ. We will earnestly and fervently beseech these lost souls to turn and look unto the Lord in faith as their eternal Savior. Yea, we will earnestly and fervently pray for these lost souls that they might "***be saved***" and "***come unto the knowledge of the truth.***" (1 Timothy 2:4)

Furthermore, with a truly broken and contrite heart, we will earnestly and fervently seek after believers who have spiritually gone away backward into sin. We will earnestly and fervently seek after them in order that we may convert them from the error of their ways, and thereby deliver them from spiritual destruction. (James 5:19-20) We will earnestly and fervently seek the restoration of these backslidden believers unto the way of righteousness through the humble repentance of their sins. Yea, we will earnestly and fervently pray for these backslidden believers that the Lord might return them unto an abundant spiritual walk.

Even so, with a truly broken and contrite heart, we will seek after the conversion of these sinners "***in the spirit of meekness.***" (Galatians 6:1) We will humbly consider ourselves, remembering that we have been tempted and have previously fallen into sin. In addition, we will humbly consider ourselves, recognizing that we could be tempted and could again fall into sin. With a truly broken and contrite heart, we will recognize that we ourselves are not above the wretchedness and wickedness of sin. Thus we will not look down with a haughty heart upon other sinners.

As those who have been spiritually restored by God's abundant grace and tender mercies, we will not strive with selfish superiority over other sinners. Rather, as the humble servants of our Lord, we will *"be gentle unto all men, apt to teach, patient, in meekness instructing those that oppose themselves; if God peradventure will give them repentance to the acknowledging of the truth; and that they may recover themselves out of the snare of the devil, who are taken captive by him at his will."* (2 Timothy 2:24-26)

Yea, with a truly broken and contrite heart over our own sin, we will seek to teach other sinners the ways of the Lord by *"speaking the truth in love."* (Ephesians 4:15) We will remember the horrible pit and miry clay into which we had previously fallen. We will remember how the cords of our own sins had bound us in spiritual bondage. We will remember, not only the stubbornness, but also the fragileness of our own heart. Even so, we will remember how the Lord, in the multitude of His tender mercies and loving kindnesses, disciplined us unto repentance, drew us unto Himself, and delivered us from the corruption and bondage of our sin. Thus with a truly broken and contrite heart, we will be apt to teach other sinners with a spirit of meekness, gentleness, and patience.

Such is the first commitment of a truly broken and contrite heart – *"Then will I teach transgressors thy ways."* Even so, such is the assurance of a truly broken and contrite heart – *"And sinners shall be converted unto thee."* The commitment of a truly broken and contrite heart is to teach other sinners the Lord's ways of repentance, return, restoration, and righteousness. The assurance of a truly broken and contrite is that some sinners shall indeed be converted unto the Lord.

Oh, what a wonderful assurance! If we go forth with a truly broken and contrite heart, the Holy Spirit of God will fill us with His power for ministry. Then as we go forth in the power of the Holy Spirit, sinners *will* be converted unto the Lord because our Lord *will* use a truly broken and contrite heart. Indeed, such a truly broken and contrite heart *"shall be a vessel unto honour, sanctified, and meet for the master's use, and prepared unto every good work."* (2 Timothy 2:21)

Showing Forth the Praise of the Lord

In Psalm 51:14-15 David expressed his second commitment unto the Lord, saying, *"Deliver me from bloodguiltiness, O God, thou God of my salvation: and my tongue shall sing aloud of thy righteousness. O Lord, open thou my lips; and my mouth shall shew forth thy praise."* Having experienced the Lord's forgiving mercy, cleansing grace, transforming power, restored fellowship, abundant joy, spiritual guidance, and upholding love, David committed himself to praise and exalt the Lord continually for what the Lord had so graciously and mercifully done for him.

Often we speak forth the complaints of our lives rather than show forth the praises of our Lord. Yet with a truly broken and contrite heart, we will recognize the abundant grace and tender mercies that we have received from the Lord our God. Even so, with a truly broken and contrite heart, we will be quick to sing aloud of our Lord's righteousness and to show forth all His praise.

Our testimony will be that of David from Psalm 40:2-3 – *"He brought me up also out of an horrible pit, out of the miry clay, and set my feet upon a rock, and established my goings. And he hath put a new song in my mouth, even praise unto our God: many shall see it, and fear, and shall trust in the LORD."* Again our testimony will be that of David from Psalm 40:5 – *"Many, O LORD my God, are thy wonderful works which thou hast done, and thy thoughts which are to us-ward: they cannot be reckoned* [counted] *up in order unto thee: if I would declare and speak of them, they are more than can be numbered."*

In fact, that we should show forth His praises is one of the reasons that the Lord our God and Savior delivered us from our sins and chose us as His people. 1 Peter 2:9-10 proclaims, *"But ye are a chosen generation, a royal priesthood, an holy nation, a peculiar people; that ye should shew forth the praises of him who hath called you out of darkness into his marvellous light: which in time past were not a people, but are now the people of God: which had not obtained mercy, but now have obtained mercy."*

Yea, in Isaiah 12:1-6 our Lord Himself speaks of the songs and praises that will spring forth from our lips in the day of our forgiveness and cleansing. There He declares, *"And in that day thou shalt say, O LORD, I will praise thee: though thou wast angry with me, thine anger is turned away, and thou comfortedst me. Behold, God is my salvation; I will trust, and not be afraid: for the LORD JEHOVAH is my strength and my song; he also is become my salvation. Therefore with joy shall ye draw water out of the wells of salvation. And in that day shall ye say, Praise the LORD, call upon his name, declare his doings among the people, make mention that his name is exalted. Sing unto the LORD; for he hath done excellent things: this is known in all the earth. Cry out and shout, thou inhabitant of Zion: for great is the Holy One of Israel in the midst of thee."*

Such is the sacrifice that the Lord our God is seeking from us – the sacrifice of a truly broken and contrite heart singing aloud and showing forth His righteousness and His praises. David recognized this truth in Psalm 51:15-17, saying, *"O Lord, open thou my lips; and my mouth shall shew forth thy praise. For thou desirest not sacrifice; else would I give it: thou delightest not in burnt offering. The sacrifices of God are a broken spirit: a broken and a contrite heart, O God, thou wilt not despise."* Even so, Hebrews 13:15 gives the instruction, *"By him therefore* [that is – by Jesus Christ our Lord and Savior] *let us offer the sacrifice of praise to God continually, that is, the fruit of our lips giving thanks to his name."*

Finally, David closed Psalm 51 with a prayer for the Lord's people and with an assurance of the Lord's pleasure. In verse 18 David lifted up his prayer unto the Lord, saying, *"Do good in thy good pleasure unto Zion: build thou the walls of Jerusalem."* David prayed for the Lord to do good unto His people and to build up His people. He prayed for the Lord to do this *in His good pleasure*. Therefore, since our Lord finds pleasure in a truly broken and contrite heart, we can fully expect that He will do good and build up those who come before Him with a truly broken and contrite heart.

Even so, in verse 19 David expressed his assurance in the Lord, saying, *"**Then shalt thou be pleased with the sacrifices of righteousness, with burnt offering and whole burnt offering: then shall they offer bullocks upon thine altar.**"* In verse 16 David had recognized that the Lord our God does not desire or delight in our outward sacrifices and service when we are walking in sin. Rather, according to the truth of verse 17, the Lord our God desires and delights in a truly broken and contrite heart of repentance over our sin. *Then, after* we have returned unto Him with a truly broken and contrite heart, the Lord our God will be pleased with our outward sacrifices and service of righteousness. *First*, He desires and delights in our broken and contrite heart. *Then* He desires and delights in our outward service of righteousness.

Is our Lord pleased with us? How often do we sin against the Lord our God? How often then do we come unto His throne of grace with a truly broken and contrite heart over our sin? How often do we seek for the Lord's forgiveness of our sins, wholly resting upon the multitude of His tender mercies? How often do we seek for a thorough cleansing from the Lord? How often do we acknowledge our transgressions without any excuses or blame shifting? How often do we recognize the fullness of our sin's offense against the Lord our God? How often do we accept His chastening against our sin without complaint, anger, or bitterness? How often do we acknowledge the desperate wickedness and utter wretchedness of our own sinful, ungodly character? How often do we seek for the Lord to search and try our hearts to reveal any wicked ways therein?

How much then do we rest with full assurance and hope in the cleansing power of God's grace and Christ's blood? How much do we turn from the empty, carnal pleasures of our sin in order to seek true, lasting joy in our Lord? How much do we desire and pray that the Lord will transform our very character, to create in us a clean heart and renew in us a right spirit? How much do we fervently pray for the Lord graciously to restore us unto the spiritual blessings of His fellowship? How much have we committed ourselves to teach other sinners the ways of the Lord that they might be converted unto Him? How much have we committed ourselves to sing out and show forth the righteousness and praises of the Lord our God?

A Sinners Prayer

Oh, Lord, teach me to have a truly broken and contrite heart over my sin. Wherever there may be a resistance to righteousness, a regarding of sin, a rebellion in heart, then break my heart. Teach me to receive with meekness the conviction of Thy Holy Word upon my heart. Convict me to acknowledge my sins – not to excuse them, or to shift the blame. Teach me to humbly confess my sins and to plead for the forgiveness and cleansing of my unrighteousness. Oh, Lord, I thank Thee for Thy gracious and merciful promise of forgiveness and cleansing. According to the abundance of Thy grace and the multitude of Thy tender mercies, use the living power of Thy Holy Word to renew the spirit of my mind and to transform the character of my heart and life. Oh, that I might not sin against Thee without concern and might not regard iniquity in my heart! Create in me a clean heart and a right spirit that I might have a spiritual sensitivity against sin and a hunger and thirst after righteousness. Oh, Lord, I thank Thee for the promise of a restored fellowship with Thee and for the gracious blessing of that fellowship. Teach me ever to long for and submit to the holy influence, godly wisdom, and victorious power of Thy Holy Spirit. Teach me to yield and to obey. Then use me to reach others for Thee, and fill my mouth with Thy praises. Amen.

Isaiah 66:1-2, 5

Thus saith the LORD,
The heaven is my throne,
and the earth is my footstool:
where is the house that ye build unto me?
And where is the place of my rest?
For all those things hath mine hand made,
and all those things have been,
saith the LORD:
but to this man will I look,
even to him that is poor and of a contrite spirit,
and trembleth at my word.

Hear the word of the LORD,
ye that tremble at his word;
Your brethren that hated you,
that cast you out for my name's sake, said,
Let the LORD be glorified;
but he shall appear to your joy,
and they shall be ashamed.

Chapter Twenty

To This Man Will I Look

In the closing portion of Isaiah 66:2, the Lord our God and Creator, the sovereign Lord of heaven and earth, declares, "***But to this man will I look, even to him that is poor and of a contrite spirit, and trembleth at my word.***" Herein the Lord our God indicates that He will look with favor upon and fellowship toward those who are of a poor (humble) and a contrite spirit. Furthermore, the Lord our God indicates that those who are of a poor (humble) and a contrite spirit will demonstrate this spirit by trembling at His Holy Word.

Already from Psalm 51 we have considered the relationship of a broken and contrite heart *toward sin*. Now from Isaiah 66:1-6 we shall consider the relationship of a humble and contrite heart *toward God's Word*. According to the truth and teaching of God's Word, the spirit of godly humility is absolutely necessary for spiritual revival. Even so, a broken and contrite heart over our sin is necessary for us *to enter into* the path of spiritual revival. Yet a humble and contrite spirit toward God's Word is necessary for us *to continue in* the path of spiritual revival. So then, what are the ingredients and characteristics of a humble and contrite spirit toward God's Word?

Our Lord's primary thrust in Isaiah 66:1-6 was to present His rebuke against those who made sacrifices and gave service unto Him outwardly, while maintaining a disobedient and stubborn spirit toward Him. In the closing line of verse 3, our Lord revealed their true spiritual character, saying, "***Yea, they have chosen their own ways, and their soul*** *delighteth in their abominations."* To this He added in verse 4, saying, *"I also will choose their delusions, and will bring their fears upon them; because when I called, none did answer; when I spake, they did not hear: but they did evil before mine eyes, and chose that in which I delighted not."* When the Lord spoke, they rebelled against His Word. Thus our Lord pronounced His chastening against them.

However, in contrast to those of a stubborn and rebellious spirit, our Lord presented His commendation for those who maintained a humble and contrite spirit before Him. These individuals did not rebel against His Word. Rather, they trembled at His Word. Thus our Lord pronounced His favor upon them in verse 2, saying, *"But to this man will I look, even to him that is poor and of a contrite spirit, and trembleth at my word."* To this He added in verse 5, saying, *"Hear the word of the LORD, ye that tremble at his word; Your brethren that hated you, that cast you out for my name's sake, said, Let the LORD be glorified: but he shall appear to your joy, and they shall be ashamed."*

Standing in Awe at the Person of God's Word

In verse 1 the Lord our God began His rebuke, saying, *"Thus saith the LORD, The heaven is my throne, and the earth is my footstool: where is the house that ye build unto me? And where is the place of my rest?"* With these opening words, the Lord our God proclaimed His infinite greatness. He proclaimed that He is the Lord God of heaven and earth. He proclaimed that He is the Lord God of heaven, in that His throne, the seat of His sovereign authority, is there. He proclaimed that He is the Lord God of earth, in that the earth is His footstool. All the inhabitants of the earth are under His feet. We are all under the rule of His sovereign authority.

In addition, our Lord proclaimed that He is the Creator God of the heaven and the earth, and of all that is in them. In the opening portion of verse 2 our Lord declared, *"For all those things hath mine hand made, and all those things have been, saith the LORD."* In like manner, in Isaiah 48:13 He proclaimed, *"Mine hand also hath laid the foundation of the earth, and my right hand hath spanned the heavens: when I call unto them, they stand up together."* He is our Lord God, our Creator God, the great God on high.

Even so, Psalm 145:3 declares, *"Great is the LORD, and greatly to be praised; and his greatness is unsearchable."* *"The heaven and heaven of heavens"* cannot contain Him. (1 Kings 8:27) *"The LORD is high above all nations, and his glory above the heavens."* (Psalm 113:4) *"Who is like unto the LORD our God, who dwelleth on high, who humbleth himself to behold the things that are in heaven, and in the earth!"* (Psalm 113:4) Indeed, the Lord our God is so great that He must humble Himself and stoop down even to observe the things that are in heaven.

Furthermore, the Lord our God is so great that He can do whatever He pleases, whenever He pleases, however He pleases. No person and no force can stay His hand. He is the everlasting Sovereign of heaven and earth. Even so, Psalm 115:3 declares, *"But our God is in the heavens: he hath done whatsoever he hath pleased."* To this Psalm 93:1-2 adds, *"The LORD reigneth, he is clothed with majesty; the LORD is clothed with strength, wherewith he hath girded himself: the world also is stablished, that it cannot be moved. Thy throne is established of old: thou art from everlasting."*

How then should we respond to the infinite greatness of the Lord our God, the Lord our Creator and Sovereign? Psalm 96:4 gives answer, saying, *"For the LORD is great, and greatly to be praised: he is to be feared above all gods."* To this verse 9 adds, *"O worship the LORD in the beauty of holiness: fear before him, all the earth."* Again Psalm 99:1 proclaims, *"The LORD reigneth; let the people tremble: he sitteth between the cherubims; let the earth be moved."* Yet again Psalm 89:6-7 proclaims, *"For who in the heaven can be compared unto the LORD? Who among the sons of the mighty can be likened unto the LORD? God is greatly to be feared in the assembly of the saints, and to be had in reverence of all them that are about him."* Finally, Psalm 33:8 declares, *"Let all the earth fear the LORD: let all the inhabitants of the world stand in awe of him."*

We are to respond unto the infinite greatness of the Lord our God, the Lord our Creator and Sovereign, by fearing and trembling before Him. We are to respond by having Him in reverence. We are to respond by standing in awe of Him. Even so, a truly humble and contrite spirit before the Lord trembles at the Word of God because such a spirit first trembles before the God of the Word. With a truly humble and contrite spirit, we will stand in reverential, trembling awe of the Lord our God. Then with such a reverential, trembling awe of our Lord, we will tremble with reverence and submission at the truth of His Word.

Yet there are many, even among God's own people, who will not have a humble and contrite heart before Him. They will not stand in awe before the Lord their Creator and Sovereign, and they will not tremble at His true and holy Word. Yea, it was against those with just such a stubborn and rebellious spirit that the Lord our God delivered His rebuke in Isaiah 66:1-6.

In the closing portion of verse 1, after proclaiming that the heaven is His throne, and that the earth is His footstool, the Lord confronted such individuals with two questions, asking, **"Where is the house that ye build unto me? And where is the place of my rest?"** At that time, many among God's people intended to build a temple for the Lord. In itself, building such a temple for the glory of the Lord was not wrong. Yet their heart attitude in the matter was utterly rebellious.

With a stubborn and rebellious spirit, they intended to build this temple, not in order that they might worship the Lord in the beauty of holiness, but in order that they might contain Him for their own benefit. Certainly they intended to build a grand and glorious temple from the perspective of mankind. Yet from the perspective of the Lord our God, the Lord of heaven and earth, who is infinitely greater than heaven and earth, and who eternally rules over heaven and earth, it would be a mere box made with men's hands.

Furthermore, they intended to build this grand and glorious temple, not in order that the Lord's name might be honored thereby, but in order that they might manipulate the Lord's favor thereby. They intended to place a constraint upon the Lord through this temple, in order that they might use Him and His power for their own selfish purpose. In the conceit of their stubborn and rebellious spirit, they believed that they could contain, manipulate, manage, and use the infinitely great Lord God of heaven and earth.

Yet the Lord our God does not look with favor, but with fiery indignation, upon the conceit of a stubborn, rebellious spirit. Rather, He looks with favor upon the submission of a humble, contrite spirit. Therefore, we must never think that we can contain Him in a box of our own creation, that we can manipulate His hand of blessing upon our lives, or that we can manage Him and use Him for our purposes. Rather, we must ever bow with a truly humble and contrite spirit before Him, submitting ourselves under His sovereign authority. Yea, we must ever join with the spirit of psalmist from Psalm 119:120, saying, *"My flesh trembleth for fear of thee; and I am afraid of thy judgments."*

Standing in Awe at the Power of God's Word

In the opening portion of Isaiah 66:1, the Lord our God declared, *"Thus saith the LORD, The heaven is my throne, and the earth is my footstool."* Then He added in the opening portion of verse 2, *"For all those things hath mine hand made, and all those things have been, saith the LORD."* Throughout the creation account of Genesis 1, we find the phrase repeated, *"And God said, let there be. . . ."* Then we find the response, *"And it was so."*

Even so, Psalm 33:6 proclaims, *"By the word of the LORD were the heavens made; and all the host of them by the breath of his mouth."* In like manner, Hebrews 11:3 states, *"Through faith we understand that the worlds were framed by the word of God, so that things which are seen were not made of things which do appear."* This is the infinite, almighty power of God's Word. It is the power to create out of nothing.

Yet there is more. The opening portion of Isaiah 66:2 speaks, not only concerning our Lord God's work of creation, but also concerning His work of upholding. *"For all those things hath mine hand made, and all those things have been, saith the LORD."* With the two words "have been," our Lord indicates, not only that He brought all the creation into existence at the beginning, but also that He has kept that creation in existence since the beginning.

Even so, Hebrews 1:1-3 proclaims, *"**God, who at sundry times and in divers manners spake in time past unto the fathers by the prophets, hath in these last days spoken unto us by his Son, whom he hath appointed heir of all things, by whom also he made the worlds; who being the brightness of his glory, and the express image of his person, and upholding all things by the word of his power, when he had by himself purged our sins, sat down on the right hand of the Majesty on high.**"* Again this is the infinite, almighty power of God's Word. It is the power, not only to speak the creation into existence, but also to uphold all of the existing creation.

Now, for our personal lives, that same infinite, almighty power is found in the divinely inspired Scriptures, the Holy Bible that the Lord our God has graciously given to us. *"**All Scripture is given by inspiration of God.**"* (2 Timothy 3:16) Thus Hebrews 4:12 declares, *"**For the word of God is quick** [alive]**, and powerful, and sharper than any twoedged sword, piercing even to the dividing asunder of soul and spirit, and of the joints and marrow, and is a discerner of the thoughts and intents of the heart.**"* This is the power of God's Holy Word for our lives. It is the power to pierce the depths of our hearts and to discern the true character of our innermost thoughts and intentions.

Again Psalm 19:7-8 declares, *"**The law of the LORD is perfect, converting the soul: the testimony of the LORD is sure, making wise the simple. The statutes of the LORD are right, rejoicing the heart: the commandment of the LORD is pure, enlightening the eyes.**"* This also is the power of God's Holy Word for our lives. It is the power to convert our souls spiritually, to make us truly wise, to fill our hearts with true joy, and to enlighten our eyes with spiritual understanding.

Yet again in Psalm 119:11 the psalmist declared, *"**Thy word have I hid in mine heart, that I might not sin against thee.**"* Then in verse 105 he added, *"**Thy word is a lamp unto my feet, and a light unto my path.**"* This also is the power of God's Holy Word for our lives. It is the power to guard us from sin and to guide us in righteousness. And yet again Romans 15:4 declares, *"**For whatsoever**"* *things were written aforetime were written for our learning, that we through patience and comfort of the scriptures might have hope.*" This also is the power of God's Holy Word for our lives. It is the power to comfort us and to give us hope.

Finally, 2 Timothy 3:16-17 declares, "*All scripture is given by inspiration of God, and is profitable for doctrine, for reproof, for correction, for instruction in righteousness: that the man of God may be perfect, throughly furnished unto all good works.*" This also is the power of God's Holy Word for our lives. It is the power to teach us what is right, to confront us wherever we are wrong, to direct us in making things right, and to instruct us in walking aright thereafter. In all, it is the power to produce spiritual maturity in us and to prepare us unto every good work that our Lord would have us to do.

How then should we respond to the living power of God's Holy Word in our lives? In Psalm 119:161-163 the psalmist gives answer, saying, "*Princes have persecuted me without a cause: but my heart standeth in awe of thy word. I rejoice at thy word, as one that findeth great spoil. I hate and abhor lying: but thy law do I love.*" We are to respond unto the living power of God's Holy Word by standing in awe of it, trembling at its truth with a truly humble and contrite spirit and rejoicing in its truth with a loving and committed obedience.

First, with a truly humble and contrite spirit, we will tremble at and rejoice in the *conviction* of God's Word. This is seen through the example of the godly remnant in Ezra's time. Concerning them Ezra the priest stated in Ezra 9:4, "*Then were assembled unto me every one that trembled at the words of the God of Israel, because of the transgression of those that had been carried away; and I sat astonied until the evening sacrifice.*" They trembled at God's Word *because of the transgression* of the people. They trembled at the conviction of God's Word.

Second, with a truly humble and contrite spirit, we will tremble at and rejoice in the *counsel* of God's Word. This is seen through the example of Saul (Paul) at his conversion. After the Lord Jesus Christ spoke from heaven and confronted Saul on the road to Damascus, the opening portion of Acts 9:6 reports concerning Saul, "***And he trembling and astonished said, Lord, what wilt thou have me to do?***" After receiving the conviction of God's Word, he then trembled for the counsel of God's Word.

Third, with a truly humble and contrite spirit, we will tremble at and rejoice in the *commands* of God's Word. This is seen also through the example of the godly remnant in Ezra's time. In Ezra 10:3 they expressed their commitment unto the Lord, saying, "***Now therefore let us make a covenant with our God to put away all the wives, and such as are born of them, according to the counsel of my lord, and of those that tremble at the commandment of our God; and let it be done according to the law.***" After receiving the counsel of God's Word, they then trembled at the commandment of God's Word, even unto commitment and obedience.

Chapter Twenty-One

To Him that Is of a Contrite Spirit

In the closing portion of Isaiah 66:2, the Lord our God indicates that He will look with favor upon those who are of a humble and contrite spirit, trembling at His Word. As we have learned from Psalm 51, a broken and contrite heart over our sin is necessary for us *to enter into* the path of spiritual revival. Yet a humble and contrite spirit toward God's Word is necessary for us *to continue in* the path of spiritual revival. So then, what are the ingredients and characteristics of a humble and contrite spirit toward God's Word?

Submitting Ourselves to the Piercing of God's Word

From our Lord's message to His people in Isaiah 66:1-2, we have learned that trembling at God's Word includes standing in awe at the Person of God's Word and standing in awe at the power of God's Word. Our Lord's message then continued in verse 3 with a rebuke against those of His people who worshipped Him hypocritically. Therein He cried forth, "*He that killeth an ox is as if he slew a man; he that sacrificeth a lamb, as if he cut off a dog's neck; he that offereth an oblation, as if he offered swine's blood; he that burneth incense, as if he blessed an idol. Yea, they have chosen their own ways, and their soul delighteth in their abominations.*"

Indeed, these particular individuals were performing the religious services and practices that the Lord Himself had commanded in the Law of Moses. They were sacrificing the oxen and the lambs just as

He had proscribed. They were offering their oblations and burning the incense just as He had instructed. Yet the Lord did not view these religious services and practices with delight, but with disgust. He viewed their sacrificing of oxen as if they were committing the murder of a man. He viewed their offering of lambs and other sacrifices as if they were offering the carcasses of dogs and the blood of swine. He viewed their burning of incense as if they were blessing an idol. In the Lord's sight, their religious services and practices were a hateful abomination.

Yet why would the Lord disapprove so strongly against the very services and practices that He Himself had required? He did so because their hearts were not right. Although they had an external *form* of godliness, in their hearts they denied the *power* of godliness. (2 Timothy 3:5) They denied the Lord from ruling with all power over their hearts. They denied the Lord His rightful place in their hearts. Yes, they drew near unto the Lord with their mouths and honored Him with their lips; yet they had removed their hearts far from Him. (Isaiah 29:13) Thus all of their religious services and practices were empty and worthless in the sight of the Lord.

Although they appeared beautiful and righteous outwardly, yet within their hearts they were full of all hypocrisy, uncleanness, and iniquity. Outwardly they called upon the name of the Lord. Outwardly they fulfilled the religious services of the Lord. Outwardly they acted as if they delighted in the ways of the Lord. Yet in their hearts they had chosen and were delighting in the abomination of their own selfish ways. Even so, the Lord proclaimed in the closing line of Isaiah 66:3, "***Yea, they have chosen their own ways, and their soul delighteth in their abominations.***"

On the other hand, those who tremble at God's Holy Word stand in direct contrast to these hypocritical worshippers. Such individuals understand that God's Word is able to pierce unto the very depths of our innermost being. Yea, it is their understanding of this very principle that causes them to tremble at God's Word. They have truly begun to grasp the truth of Hebrews 4:12-13 – "***For the word of God is quick, and powerful, and sharper than any twoedged sword, piercing even to the dividing asunder of soul and spirit,*** *and of the joints and marrow, and is a discerner of the thoughts and intents of the heart. Neither is there any creature that is not manifest in his sight: but all things are naked and opened unto the eyes of him with whom we have to do."*

The Lord our God sees and knows even the deepest thoughts and intents of our hearts. With His living, powerful Word, He pierces our hearts through, dividing and searching every dark corner and locked closet of our soul and spirit. Furthermore, with His living, powerful Word, He discerns and tries every thought and intention that we hide within.

Thus with a truly humble and contrite spirit, we will tremble at the living power of God's Word and will submit ourselves unto the piercing work of God's Word. First, with a truly humble and contrite spirit, we will recognize that all hypocritical services and practices are spiritually empty. We will recognize that every show of godliness before men is worthless, and that only a sincere heart before the Lord is worthwhile.

Furthermore, with a truly humble and contrite spirit, we will understand the power of God's Holy Word both to divide and discern our hearts. We will tremble at the holiness of God's Word and will ask for our Lord to search our hearts and try our thoughts through His Holy Word.

Finally, with a truly humble and contrite spirit, we will submit ourselves unto the piercing conviction of God's Holy Word. We will ask for our Lord to reprove us by His Word of any wicked way that is within us. Then when such reproof is delivered, we will accept it with meekness, confess our sinful ways, and seek for our Lord to lead us through His Holy Word in correcting our lives.

Submitting Ourselves to the Purity of God's Word

In the closing line of Isaiah 66:3, the Lord our God continued His rebuke of those who worshipped Him hypocritically. Therein He said, "***Yea, they have chosen their own ways, and their soul delighteth in their abominations.***" As we have noted, these people were performing the religious services and practices that the Lord had commanded in the Law of Moses. Yet, as we have noted further, they had removed their hearts far from the Lord. The closing line of verse 3 indicates that in their hearts they had chosen their own ways rather than God's ways. Their souls were delighting in those things that the Lord considered to be a hateful abomination. They had chosen and were delighting in their own fleshly desires and selfish ways. Yes, they were performing the "right" practices in their religious services. Yet in the depths of their hearts, in the delight of their souls, and in the direction of their lives, they were choosing their own fleshly ways rather than the Lord's holy ways.

On the other hand, those who tremble at God's Holy Word do not reject the Lord's holy ways in order to follow their own selfish ways. Rather, they reject their own selfish, sinful ways in order to choose the pure, holy ways of the Lord their God. Those who tremble at God's Holy Word deny themselves, crucifying the affections and desires of their sinful flesh. They do not delight in their own will or choose their own way. In everything they delight in the Lord's will, choose to walk in the Lord's ways, and live in accord with the standard of the Lord's Word. They do not simply submit themselves unto the piercing conviction and correction of God's Word, seeking to return unto a right relationship with our Lord. They also submit themselves unto the pure truth and teaching of God's Word, seeking to grow in the righteous ways of our Lord.

Thus with a truly humble and contrite spirit, we will tremble at the living power of God's Word and will submit ourselves unto the pure truth of God's Word. We will ever pray for our Lord to guide us, guard us, and govern us by His Word, all in order that we might faithfully walk in the path of righteousness. We will ever pray for our Lord to show us His ways, teach us His paths, and lead us in His truth. (Psalm 25:4-5) We will desire ***"the sincere milk of the word"*** in order that we might grow spiritually thereby. (1 Peter 2:2) We will ever pray that our Lord might show us the wondrous truths and teachings of His Word (Psalm 119:18), in order that we might ***"grow in grace, and in the knowledge of our Lord and Saviour Jesus Christ."*** (2 Peter 3:18)

With a truly humble and contrite spirit, we will ever receive with meekness the correction and instruction of God's Word, unto the spiritual transforming of our souls. (James 1:21) With a truly humble and contrite spirit, we will ever seek for our Lord's Word to dwell in us richly in all wisdom, even unto faithful obedience. (Colossians 3:16) With a truly humble and contrite spirit, we will ever delight in our Lord's Word, meditating therein day and night. (Psalm 1:2) With a truly humble and contrite spirit, we will ever hide our Lord's Word in our hearts, that we might not sin against Him. (Psalm 119:11)

Chapter Twenty-Two

To Him that Trembleth at My Word

If we desire to walk in spiritual revival, in daily fellowship with our Lord and under the daily favor of our Lord, then we must be of a truly humble and contrite spirit, trembling at His Word. In the closing portion of Isaiah 66:2, the Lord our God declares, *"But to this man will I look, even to him that is poor and of a contrite spirit, and trembleth at my word."* Already we have considered four ingredients and characteristics of a truly humble and contrite spirit that trembles at God's Word. In this chapter, we shall consider the final two ingredients and characteristics.

Setting Our Hearts upon the Pursuit of God's Word

With the opening line of Isaiah 66:4, the Lord our God pronounced His judgment against those who worshipped Him hypocritically, saying, *"I also will choose their delusions, and will bring their fears upon them."* Then He continued with the reason for His judgment, saying, *"Because when I called, none did answer; when I spake, they did not hear: but they did evil before mine eyes, and chose that in which I delighted not."*

Herein the Lord gave three reasons for His judgment against these hypocritical worshippers. First, He would bring their fears upon them because, when He called them to draw nigh unto Him and submit their hearts before Him, they would not even answer Him. They completely and willfully ignored the Lord's call. Second, He would bring their fears upon them because, when He presented unto them the instruction of His Word, they would not hear. They were dull of hearing toward the Lord's Word. Third, He would bring their fears upon them because they did evil before His eyes and purposefully chose that in which He did not delight. They delighted in the sinful ways of their flesh and refused to walk in the ways of the Lord's delight.

On the other hand, those who tremble at God's Holy Word do not ignore the Lord's call, but eagerly draw nigh unto the Lord for fellowship with Him and in submission to Him. They are not dull of hearing toward the Lord's Word, but earnestly desire the truth of the Lord's Word in order that they might grow spiritually thereby. They do not choose to follow after the ways of sin, but energetically delight in the ways of the Lord's righteousness whereby they might walk pleasing unto the Lord. With a truly humble and contrite spirit, they set their hearts upon pursuing the God of the Word, the truth of the Word, and the righteousness of the Word.

Thus with a truly humble and contrite spirit, we will set our hearts to pursue the Lord our God, *the God of the Word*. When our Lord calls from Psalm 27:8, saying, "*Seek ye my face,*" our hearts will give answer, "*Thy face, LORD, will I seek.*" When our Lord calls from Matthew 11:29, saying, "*Take my yoke upon you, and learn of me; for I am meek and lowly in heart: and ye shall find rest unto your souls,*" our hearts will give answer, "Thy yoke, O Lord, will I take upon myself; and I will set my heart to learn of Thee." When our Lord calls from Luke 9:23, saying, "*If any man will come after me, let him deny himself, and take up his cross daily, and follow me,*" our hearts will give answer, "I will deny myself; I will take up my cross of submission daily; and I will follow Thee."

With a truly humble and contrite spirit, we will seek the Lord with our whole heart. (Psalm 119:2, 10) We will seek Him early, while He may be found. (Psalm 63:1) Our souls will thirst for the Lord our God and will follow hard after Him. (Psalm 63:1, 8) With a perfect heart and a willing mind, we will seek Him and serve Him. (1 Chronicles 28:9) With a true heart in full assurance of faith, we will draw nigh unto Him. (Hebrews 10:22) Yea, we will count it the greatest blessing that the Lord our God would draw nigh unto us as we draw nigh unto Him.

Furthermore, with a truly humble and contrite spirit, we will set our hearts to pursue *the truth of God's Word*. We will be ready, quick, hungry, glad, and attentive to hear the truth and teaching, commands and counsels, statutes and standards, precepts and principles, instructions and admonitions of God's Holy Word. We will set our hearts unto the Lord, saying, "***Blessed art thou, O LORD: teach me thy statutes.***" (Psalm 119:12) We will commit ourselves unto the Lord, saying, "***I have rejoiced in the way of thy testimonies, as much as in all riches. I will meditate in thy precepts, and have respect unto thy ways. I will delight myself in thy statutes: I will not forget thy word.***" (Psalm 119:14-16) We will lift up our prayer unto the Lord, saying, "***Open thou mine eyes, that I may behold wondrous things out of thy law.***" (Psalm 119:18)

With a truly humble and contrite spirit, our souls will break for the longing that they have toward the truth of God's Word at all times. (Psalm 119:20) We will take the truth of God's Word as our delight and our counselors. (Psalm 119:24) We will pray unto the Lord, saying, "***Teach me, O LORD, the way of thy statutes; and I shall keep it unto the end. Give me understanding, and I shall keep thy law; yea, I shall observe it with my whole heart. Make me to go in the path of thy commandments; for therein do I delight. Incline my heart unto thy testimonies, and not to covetousness.***" (Psalm 119:33-36) We will love the truth of God's Word and will meditate therein all the day. (Psalm 119:97)

Finally, with a truly humble and contrite spirit, we will set our hearts to pursue *the righteousness of God's Word*. We will direct ourselves to walk in the Word and ways of our Lord, obeying all His instruction and fleeing from all iniquity. We will cry out unto the Lord, saying, "***O that my ways were directed to keep thy statutes!***" (Psalm 119:5) We will hide God's Holy Word in our hearts in order that we might not sin against Him. (Psalm 119:11) Each day we will choose the way of our Lord's truth, turn our feet unto His testimonies, and run in the way of His commandments. (Psalm 119:30, 32, 59) We will make haste and not delay to obey our Lord's Word. (Psalm 119:60) Yea, we will commit ourselves to obey His Word "***continually for ever and ever.***" (Psalm 119:44)

With a truly humble and contrite spirit, we will refrain our feet from every evil way in order that we might obey our Lord's Word. (Psalm 119:101) Because of the spiritual understanding that we acquire through the precepts and principles of our Lord's Word, we will come to *"hate every false way."* (Psalm 119:104, 128) We will cry forth with the psalmist from Psalm 119:113, *"I hate vain thoughts: but thy law do I love."*

Setting Our Hearts upon the Perseverance of God's Word

After pronouncing His rebuke and His judgment against those who worshipped Him hypocritically, the Lord our God proclaimed His praise and His vindication for those who trembled at His Word with a truly humble and contrite spirit. In Isaiah 66:5 the Lord proclaimed with a great voice, *"Hear the word of the LORD, ye that tremble at his word; Your brethren that hated you, that cast you out for my name's sake, said, Let the LORD be glorified: but he shall appear to your joy, and they shall be ashamed."*

Herein the Lord presented His promise and assurance to those that trembled at His Holy Word. Although they had been hated and cast out by the hypocritical worshippers, the Lord their God promised that He Himself would appear and stand forth on their behalf. Indeed, the Lord our God Himself will appear unto the joy of those who tremble at His Word with a truly humble and contrite spirit. In addition, the Lord our God Himself will bring to shame all the hypocritical worshippers who pour out hatred upon the faithful.

Even so, those who tremble at God's Word not only set their hearts upon the pursuit of God's Word, but also set their hearts upon the perseverance of God's Word. Yea, they set their hearts to pursue God's Word with perseverance unto the end no matter what the cost may be. As the Lord revealed in Isaiah 66:5, those who tremble at God's Word with obedience and godly living shall suffer persecution. The unfaithful and ungodly shall hate them and shall cast them out of their company. *"Yea, and all that will live godly in Christ Jesus shall suffer persecution."* (2 Timothy 3:12)

Such hatred and persecution is a fact of godly living. Thus in John 15:18-21 our Lord Jesus Christ warned His faithful servants, saying, ***"If the world hate you, ye know that it hated me before it hated you. If ye were of the world, the world would love his own: but because ye are not of the world, but I have chosen you out of the world, therefore the world hateth you. Remember the word that I said unto you, The servant is not greater than his lord. If they have persecuted me, they will also persecute you; if they have kept my saying, they will keep yours also. But all these things will they do unto you for my name's sake, because they know not him that sent me."***

In addition, our Lord Jesus Christ warned His faithful servants in John 16:1-3, saying, ***"These things have I spoken unto you, that ye should not be offended. They shall put you out of the synagogues: yea, the time cometh, that whosoever killeth you will think that he doeth God service. And these things will they do unto you, because they have not known the Father, nor me."*** Yea, in Isaiah 66:5 the Lord reminded those who trembled at His Word, saying, ***"Your brethren that hated you, that cast you out for my name's sake, said, Let the LORD be glorified."*** Indeed, those who worship the Lord hypocritically will actually believe that they are glorifying the Lord and doing God service when they cast out and kill the faithful, godly, humble servants of the Lord. Oh, how deeply our fleshly hearts will deceive us when we walk and worship in hypocrisy!

So then, let us flee this walk and worship of hypocrisy. Rather, let us follow after a walk and worship of humility. With a truly humble and contrite spirit, let us pursue hard after the Lord our God and His Holy Word. Yet let us ever remember that our Lord never promised that a godly walk would be an easy walk. In fact, He has specifically warned us that a walk of humble godliness will be a walk of heavy tribulation. Even so, those who tremble at God's Word with a truly humble and contrite spirit will endure in faithfulness. They will continue in the things that they have learned and been assured of from God's Word. (2 Timothy 3:14) They will fight a good fight. They will finish the course that the Lord has set before them. They will keep the faith. They will set their hearts upon the perseverance of God's Word.

Yet what will motivate and sustain such perseverance and faithfulness in the daily tribulations and persecutions of life? Isaiah 66:5 provides a two-fold answer. In the first place, we are given the assurance that in the end our Lord shall appear unto our joy. In the closing line of Isaiah 66:5, our Lord forcefully declared unto those who tremble at His Word, "***But He*** [the Lord God of heaven and earth Himself] ***shall appear to your joy.***"

Even so, in Matthew 5:10-12 our Lord Jesus Christ proclaimed, "***Blessed are they which are persecuted for righteousness' sake: for theirs is the kingdom of heaven. Blessed are ye, when men shall revile you, and persecute you, and shall say all manner of evil against you falsely, for my sake. Rejoice, and be exceeding glad:*** [Why?] ***for great is your reward in heaven: for so persecuted they the prophets which were before you.***"

Again in Luke 6:22-23 He proclaimed, "***Blessed are ye, when men shall hate you, and when they shall separate you from their company, and shall reproach you, and cast out your name as evil, for the Son of man's sake. Rejoice ye in that day, and leap for joy:*** [Why?] ***for, behold, your reward is great in heaven: for in the like manner did their fathers unto the prophets.***"

Yet again in 1 Peter 4:12-14 God's Word proclaims, "***Beloved, think it not strange concerning the fiery trial which is to try you, as though some strange thing happened unto you: but rejoice,*** [Why?] ***inasmuch as ye are partakers of Christ's sufferings; that, when his glory shall be revealed, ye may be glad also with exceeding joy. If ye be reproached for the name of Christ, happy are ye;*** [Why?] ***for the spirit of glory and of God resteth upon you: on their part he is evil spoken of, but on your part he is glorified.***"

This is the means by which those who tremble at God's Word with a truly humble and contrite spirit are to be motivated and sustained unto persevering faithfulness. We are to be motivated and sustained by the great reward that our Lord will give us in heaven. Furthermore, we are to be motivated and sustained by the exceeding joy that we shall have when our Lord returns. Finally, we are to be motivated and sustained by the fact that the Lord our God is glorified in our faithfulness.

In the second place, we are given the assurance that in the end our Lord shall judge those who persecute us. Again in the closing line of Isaiah 66:5, our Lord forcefully declared to those who tremble at His Word, "***And they*** [the hypocritical worshippers who persecute the Lord's faithful servants] ***shall be ashamed.***" To this verse 6 adds, "***A voice of noise from the city, a voice from the temple, a voice of the LORD that rendereth recompence to his enemies.***"

In like manner, 2 Thessalonians 1:6-10 declares, "***Seeing it is a righteous thing with God to recompense tribulation to them that trouble you; and to you who are troubled rest with us, when the Lord Jesus shall be revealed from heaven with his mighty angels, in flaming fire taking vengeance on them that know not God, and that obey not the gospel of our Lord Jesus Christ: who shall be punished with everlasting destruction from the presence of the Lord, and from the glory of his power; when he shall come to be glorified in his saints, and to be admired in all them that believe (because our testimony among you was believed) in that day.***"

Chapter Twenty-Three

Humble Yourselves Therefore

The primary purpose and premise of this book has been to focus our attention upon the principle that Biblical humility is *absolutely necessary* for spiritual revival. Indeed, the ground of spiritual revival *is* the ground of Biblical humility; and the ground of Biblical humility *is* the ground of spiritual revival. Without Biblical humility an individual cannot enter into the path of spiritual revival; and when an individual turns aside from Biblical humility, his progress along the path of spiritual revival will be lost.

"For thus saith the high and lofty One that inhabiteth eternity, whose name is Holy; I dwell in the high and holy place, with him also that is of a contrite and humble spirit, to revive the spirit of the humble, and to revive the heart of the contrite ones." (Isaiah 57:15)

"But he giveth more grace. Wherefore he saith, God resisteth the proud, but giveth grace unto the humble. Submit yourselves therefore to God. Resist the devil, and he will flee from you. Draw nigh to God, and he will draw nigh to you. Cleanse your hands, ye sinners; and purify your hearts, ye double minded. Be afflicted, and mourn, and weep: let your laughter be turned to mourning, and your joy to heaviness. Humble yourselves in the sight of the Lord, and he shall lift you up." (James 4:6-10)

"If my people, which are called by my name, shall humble themselves, and pray, and seek my face, and turn from their wicked ways; then will I hear from heaven, and will forgive their sin, and will heal their land." (2 Chronicles 7:14)

"The sacrifices of God are a broken spirit: a broken and a contrite heart, O God, thou wilt not despise." (Psalm 51:17)

". . . But to this man will I look, even to him that is poor and of a contrite spirit, and trembleth at my word." (Isaiah 66:2b)

If we desire spiritual revival, let us humble ourselves. Let us humble ourselves to repent of any sinful iniquity and stubborn rebellion in our lives. Let us humble ourselves to plead for and trust in our Lord's abundant grace for our lives. Let us humble ourselves to deny all self-will and to submit ourselves wholly unto our Lord's will. Let us humble ourselves to tremble at the truth of God's Holy Word with a life of faithful obedience. Let us humble ourselves to depend wholly upon the power of our Lord's might for spiritual victory. Let us humble ourselves to give all glory and honor unto the Lord our God and Savior. To those who will humble themselves, the Lord our God has *certainly promised* His work of spiritual revival in their lives. To those who will humble themselves, spiritual revival is *divinely assured*.

"Humble yourselves therefore under the mighty hand of God, that he may exalt you in due time: casting all your care upon him; for he careth for you. Be sober, be vigilant; because your adversary the devil, as a roaring lion, walketh about, seeking whom he may devour: whom resist stedfast in the faith, knowing that the same afflictions are accomplished in your brethren that are in the world. But the God of all grace, who hath called us unto his eternal glory by Christ Jesus, after that ye have suffered a while, make you perfect, stablish, strengthen, settle you. To him be glory and dominion for ever and ever. Amen." (1 Peter 5:6-11)

Also Available From

Shepherding the Flock Ministries
www.shepherdingtheflock.com

GOD'S WISDOM FOR MARRIAGE & THE HOME

A comprehensive study of what the Word of God teaches about marriage and the home, including chapters on:
The Priority of Marriage
The Permanency of Marriage
The Purpose of Marriage
Cleaving unto Thy Wife (Parts 1 & 2)
An Help Meet for Him (Parts 1 & 2)
One-Flesh Unity
(446 pages)

THE TENDER MERCIES OF THE LORD
COMFORT IN OUR LORD'S TENDER CARE

A biblical study concerning the Lord's tender mercies toward His own in order to provide spiritual confidence, courage, and comfort through the truth of our Lord's tender care. *(127 pages)*

Also Available From

Shepherding the Flock Ministries
www.shepherdingtheflock.com

The GOD'S OWN WORD Booklet Series

The "God's Own Word" booklet series is intended to reveal only God's own Word on a particular matter. Each booklet provides a compilation of Biblical passages on a particular subject and categorizes those passages under a set of headings related to that subject. In addition, portions of each passage are highlighted in bold italics in order to point out the parts of the passage that are the most relevant to the subject. In this manner, the reader is instructed *by God's own Word*. I pray that these booklets may spiritually edify, exhort, and encourage your heart.

GOD'S OWN WORD
To Those Who Are Mistreated

Chapter Contents
(63 pages)

Do Good to Those Who Mistreat You
Love Your Enemies
Maintain a Tender Heart and
a Forgiving Spirit
Rejoice When You Suffer for Christ's Sake
Wait with Patience upon the Lord's
Deliverance
Trust the Lord to Repay Those
Who Mistreat You

Also Available From

Shepherding the Flock Ministries
www.shepherdingtheflock.com

GOD'S OWN WORD
On The Fear of the Lord

Chapter Contents
(82 pages)

The Fear of the Lord
The Terror of the Lord –
Because of His Glory
The Fear of God's People –
Because His Hand Is with Them
Learning to Fear the Lord
The Benefits of Fearing the Lord
If You Will Not Fear the Lord
The Terror of the Lord –
Because of Our Sin

GOD'S OWN WORD
On Our Fears

Chapter Contents
(80 pages)

Fear Thou Not
Fear in the Midst of Affliction
I Will Fear No Evil
Afraid of Man
Delivered from Fear
Fear as a Judgment from the Lord

Made in the USA
Lexington, KY
19 May 2017